OTHER
PEOPLE
MY AGE ARE
—ALREADY—
GROWN
UP

OTHER PEOPLE MY AGE ARE ALREADY GROWN UP

Cliff Schimmels

OLIVER
NELSON

A Division of Thomas Nelson Publishers
Nashville

Published in Nashville, Tennessee, by Oliver-Nelson Books, a division of Thomas Nelson, Inc., Publishers, and distributed in Canada by Lawson Falle, Ltd., Cambridge, Ontario.

Printed in the United States of America.

Library of Congress Cataloging-in-Publication Data

Schimmels, Cliff.
    Other people my age are already grown up / Cliff Schimmels.
      p.   cm.
    ISBN 0-8407-9597-1 (pbk.)
    1. Meditations.   I. Title.
BV4832.2.S2785   1992
242—dc20   91–29714
                                          CIP

1 2 3 4 5 6 — 97 96 95 94 93 92

To Mom
In celebration
of
eighty years
of
wit and wisdom and life well lived.

Anybody who can call me son
has to have a sense of humor.

CONTENTS

Other People My Age
Are Already Grown Up

Alyssa, my three-year-old granddaughter, leads me through analysis. We were walking in the park, just the two of us, when I, in grandfather fashion, asked, "What do you want to be when you grow up?"

"I want to be a ballerina," she told me, and we stopped by a bench where she could brace herself, and I hummed so she could show me a ballerina's pose.

And we dreamed, the two of us, of a time way off in an unknown but possible future, when she would swirl across the stage and bring magic movement to the music of the *Nutcracker Suite*.

Alyssa broke the silence that was cushioning our dream, "What do you want to be when you grow up, Grandpa?"

I told her I wanted to be a ballplayer, and I dreamed of a time way off in an impossible future when I would catch Nolan Ryan's fastball for the last strike of the last out of the last inning of a no-hitter, and I dreamed of a time when I would dig in, face-to-face with ace relief pitcher Lee Smith, and challenge him with power against heat.

Maybe there is a difference between the dreams of a child and an old coot. Maybe her dream has a chance and mine doesn't. But you wouldn't take mine away from me just because of that, would you?

Perhaps I should dream more realistically—of a time when I would stand in front of a crowd and make a speech, but I've done that. Of a time when I would write a book, but I've done that. In my world, as in a child's, I would rather dream about the things I haven't done than the things I have.

If I ever get to the point that within my dreams my past is more exciting than my future, I fear that then I will be a grown up, and I will have to act like one. I won't be able to play with puppies, or walk through puddles, or catch June bugs, or lie on my back to watch clouds, or chew my pencils, or lick the cream filling before I eat the cookie.

If that's where being grown up is, I don't want to go. I don't ever want to lose my ability to play or to dream like a child or to believe that my Father can make everything right.

Thoughts of Joy

As I see it, there is a difference between pleasure and joy. Pleasure is the passion of the moment, while joy stays for the duration. Pleasure hangs on the humps, while joy fills the gaps. Pleasure flits from event to event, while joy settles in.

There are pleasurable thoughts and thoughts of joy. Pleasurable thoughts grab us by the shoulders, shake us a bit, and throw us back into the arena bruised but excited. Thoughts of joy sneak in by the back door, light up a remote corner of our minds, and give a twinkle to our faces that those around us see but can't understand.

Most books are about pleasure and pleasurable thoughts—history-changing events and ideas that direct the course of humanity. And I am richer for them.

I offer this little volume, however, as a tribute to thoughts of joy—those little moments of mind activity, too unassuming to remember and too entertaining to forget—those little flashes of brilliance that hit us when we are waiting for the train to pass or when we're blocked by road construction, or when we are lying in bed waiting for our minds to get as sleepy as our bodies.

If I have done a good job of identifying these moments and capturing them, there shouldn't be anything in this book that is shocking, informative, or even new. These little thoughts aren't really mine. Like the waves of the sea, they are too restless and too precious to be possessed. Yet, they belong to us all.

The Problem with Good Advice Is a Short Memory

"Mind your manners," my mother said. "Say 'yes ma'am and no ma'am,' and don't take the biggest piece of pie."

At the time, that sounded like good instruction—even more than instruction—a philosophy of life. But after I had been away from home and mother for more than thirty minutes, I forgot every word of it and went back to my old crude ways.

"Love your neighbor," the preacher said. "Pray for those who persecute you, and don't gossip."

At the time, that sounded like good instruction too—another philosophy of life. But thirty minutes after somebody said "Amen," I forgot every word of it and went back to my old crude ways.

"Eat more vegetables," the doctor said. "Watch out for salt and cut down on the meat."

At the time, that sounded like good instruction— yet another philosophy of life. But thirty minutes after paying the bill I couldn't remember which was more and what was less.

When I am in the presence of advice, I'm a good listener. I open my ears, close myself to distractions, and absorb the truth with appropriate degrees of guilt. The problem is that about thirty minutes later, when the advice has cooled a bit and it's time to make some important life decision, I just can't remember what it is I am supposed to do.

Poor memory is a nuisance anytime. You have to have bigger pockets to carry around all those letters you forgot to mail. You can't wear a good-looking ring because you've always got some piece of string wrapped around your finger as a reminder. You can't call home when you're lost because you don't have the number. Poor memory is a particular liability when it comes to good advice. People who stand around and watch you misbehave say, "tsk, tsk," as if they think you're rebellious and antisocial, when all the time the problem is simply that you have forgotten.

My solution to this problem is portable advice. At first, I just wrote every philosophical tidbit down and carried it in my wallet. But on an active day, I found myself making so many decisions and reaching and grabbing so often that I almost wore my trousers out. Next, I tried writing the good advice on my palms, on my cuffs, and on the bands of my underwear. But that brought back the distasteful memories of my junior high days when I learned to cheat in school.

Now I have stumbled upon the perfect portable transporter of good advice: T-shirts. T-shirt wisdom is already something of an accepted form of communication. Every day I meet hundreds of people who have their philosophies of life, or at least philosophies of the moment, emblazoned in some kind of pithy statement across their chests. Not long ago, I heard of a fellow who had compiled a book of T-shirt wit and wisdom appropriate for study at the graduate level.

Since such activity is already in vogue, it would seem logical that we could take the next step and start wearing good advice around on our chests. This would end the pain of trying to remember and the agony that comes from forgetting.

Perhaps I should reprint the thoughts in this book on my T-shirts. Then I could travel through life living out all of my mother's expectations, and I wouldn't have to stop all the time to explain my strange behavior to the people I meet.

4

Real Heroes Autograph Free

The world is filled with two kinds of people: big people and little people. Almost everybody in the world qualifies as a big people.

I learned that truth when I was an honest but naive reporter working for a weekly newspaper in a small, country town in West Texas. One week I accomplished the reporter's dream and discovered the reporter's nightmare. I wrote everything that was newsy. I covered all the stories. I had stories about the rain and wind; I had stories about the increase in tractor prices and the decrease in cotton prices; I had stories about the junior high honor roll; I had stories about students home from college; and I had stories about who had come to town to have Sunday dinner with whom.

I had it all, but I still didn't have enough. There was more newspaper to fill than I had stories. Because I knew that the publisher would not be too happy about running an edition of the paper filled with white space, I consulted him. In other words, I whined. "There is nothing left to write."

In his crusty, country manner, he took me to the window, which looked out over Main Street and served as our connection to the real world, and asked, "What do you see?"

"People," I answered, rather pleased with my ability to discern such things.

"Let me tell you an important truth," he said, using that kind of fatherly tone that fakes kindness beneath obvious impatience. "Every one of those people is an important person with an interesting story. If you are any kind of newspaper person, you will go out and discover some of those stories."

Prepared to prove him wrong and to show him up as a crusty old idealist, which is the very worst kind of idealist, I went out armed with my pencil and notebook, and accosted the first uninteresting-looking person I could find. I knew the man only slightly. As best as I could tell, his job in life was to go to the drugstore each morning, drink coffee, and make suggestions about how the high school football team could be improved—if only the coach were as smart as he was.

I approached this man and with the best of interviewing skills, I asked, "There isn't anything interesting in your life, is there?"

"No," he answered rather emphatically, and I started back into the office to shoot down one more idealist. "Wait a minute," the man said, as I was walking away. "I do play the bagpipes. Is that interesting?"

In that little spot in West Texas, bagpipes are about as common as dress shoes in a fiddlers contest, so I answered incredulously, "You what?"

"I play the bagpipes," he responded rather smirkly.

"There aren't any bagpipes west of St. Louis," I told him, as if I were an expert on bagpipes.

"I have some up in my house in my bathtub right now," he assured me.

I did find the bagpipes soaking in his bathtub. I took pictures of this man in Smalltown, Texas, dressed in his kilt, and I wrote a three-column story, which was lifted and carried in bigger newspapers and even won an award for unusual reporting. The bagpipe player himself became famous, at least in our little town in West Texas, and he spent his days going around autographing the original story for the people who had clipped it out of the paper.

In all that, I learned an important lesson. Almost every person I meet qualifies as a big people, and each one deserves our interest, our attention, and our respect.

Marge, my next door neighbor, is a big person in the world of evangelism; but since she only preaches to one person at a time, no one much knows it. The people she ministers to with word and homemade cookies say that she is the greatest, and that's good enough for me.

Roger, the guy who lives in the house behind mine, is a big person in the world of sports. But since he only plays in the back yard with his own children, no one much knows it. His children tell me that he is the greatest, and that's good enough for me.

Elizabeth, my student, is a big person in the world of literature. But because she only reads her poetry to her roommate, no one much knows it. Her roommate says she is the greatest, and that's good enough for me.

The most interesting thing about all these everyday heroes is that they don't think they are big people.

On the other hand, there are a few human types who are little people. Little people are just like big people, except they think they are big people, and that makes them little people.

Little people usually lurk around in the shadows of those "Professions of High Profile." Because people gawk at them all day long, like watching monkeys in a zoo, little people forget who they are and begin to think of themselves as important. They parade around, make radical statements to the newspaper, and charge for their autographs.

If I wanted to go for the tears, I would tell a story of some little boy who picked out some sports hero from the public bog. He not only admired this hero; but in his back yard he even imagined that he was this hero and played the game as his hero would.

Finally, our little boy gets the opportunity of a lifetime to meet his hero. Through perseverance and a bruise from the crowd, he comes face-to-face with this man that he admires so much; and in boy-like worship he asks for an autograph. Alas, the hero charges for such a thing, and the boy goes away sad.

I suppose we should feel sorry for the little boy and for the hurt that he has endured. But one thing we have to accept is that the little boy did get the chance to learn an important, though painful, lesson. On the other hand, I feel sorry for the "hero." He probably didn't learn much from his encounter with the boy.

The lesson for all of us is obvious. The first requirement of being a hero is not to think that you are one.

5

Aged in the Vat
of Life

I am not twenty-one years old. I am not even thirty-nine years old, or forty, or fifty. I'm above all that now, and I'm not afraid to admit it.

I don't have much call to show my ID card anymore. I have ample evidence of my years. I have gray hairs, and each one is an entry in the diary of parenting. Teething and earaches, childhood pneumonia, bike wrecks, piano recitals, and the innocent orations of children at scout meetings and school activities—such triumphs and traumas are all a part of the color of my hair these days.

I have bifocals, and each glance through the higher power recalls a book review in the library of a lifetime. Reading *Treasure Island* in the sunbeams that leaked through the holes in the barn roof one afternoon, covering all the Old Testament in a four-day period while on vacation in the Sierras, pouring through the time-worn and dusty volumes of Seneca, Quintilian, Tacitus, and Ovid during the scholarly period of my life—such experiences, vicarious and otherwise, are reflected in how my eyes work these days.

I have a sore knee, and every twinge is a chapter in a personal travelogue. The evening I ran six miles in the red clay and moonlight of rural Brazil, the day I took four laps around the famous speedway in Indianapolis, the time I fell off a donkey somewhere in the Ozarks—such adventures are all a part of my gait these days.

I have liver spots, and every dark blotch is worth a chuckle. The day I tried to learn to water ski, and the kids laughed themselves silly at my futile attempt; the hot August afternoon I ran out of gas and had to walk four miles on the interstate; the time I spaded up the whole yard to prepare for a new lawn as a special surprise to my wife Mary, only to discover that in my zeal I had killed her rhubarb plants—such comedy is all a part of my hands and arms these days.

I wear all these marks and bear these weaknesses as badges of merit. I have decided to look at them not as the blemishes of age, but as the reminders of an active life.

Occasionally, I catch a glimpse of the younger set dashing through life with their purposes hanging out like wagging tongues. They have important decisions to make, business deals to consummate, and unknown futures to explore. I don't envy them.

I hear of people my age who wish they were younger, but I won't do that. To be younger, I might have to cull out some of the experiences I have had along the way, and I wouldn't know how to make the cuts. It isn't a tragedy to have reached my age. The tragedy would be to get to my age and not have lived enough enroute.

Joshua and Caleb Wandered Too

You remember the story. It's one of the classic tales from the Old Testament. The Israelites had moved out of Egypt in a hurry, just having time to grab a few belongings and the unrisen bread. They knew what they had to do. They were to take hostile control of the Promised Land, but they just didn't quite have the strategy to do it. As usual in big business decisions, timing was a key factor. Moses, the CEO, appointed a committee of twelve to research the project.

This ad hoc group, called spies, took a quick trip to check out the possibilities of this new location.

When they got home they filed their report. Shammua, Shaphat, Igal, Hoshea, Palti, Gaddiel, Gaddi, Ammiel, Sethur, Nahbi, Geuel, Caleb, and Joshua, all highly respected company men, reported that the land of promise was indeed bountiful and plentiful. They even brought home visual aids to illustrate the point. And the members of the board oohed and ahhed at the sight.

"But," the ad hoc committee continued to report, "the people over there won't take kindly to our coming in, and they're big and tough. Real giants, in fact."

The members of the board, when they heard this, said, "Ummm." And they began to weigh the advantages of prudence and caution instead of haste.

There were two upstarts, Joshua and Caleb, on the ad hoc committee, and they urged immediate action. They suggested confidence and a bold move. But the board said, "Ummm," considered conventional wisdom, and voted for caution.

God, who was superintending the whole project, favored the bolder approach. And He was so angered by the action of the board—their inaction—that He put the whole project on hold for forty years.

That was that. The whole bunch wandered around in a downtrend for forty years eating manna instead of grapes and living in tents instead of country estates. The operative point here is that those two upstarts, Joshua and Caleb, who had pleaded for the bold approach in the first place, had to wander too.

Have you ever wondered if those chaps, sometime

15

during that forty years, didn't draw in their breath, stamp their feet, gesture widely, use their best junior high whine, and say, "That's not fair."

Of course it wasn't fair! But that's the first lesson in the pursuit of happiness. Life isn't fair.

Some thoughtless clod leaves watermelon rinds in the park, so the village passes a law prohibiting watermelons in the park. Some cheapskate cad doesn't chip in to the coffee fund, so now the management goes to a pay-by-cup dispenser. Some greedy goat sues for more than a reasonable settlement, so my insurance fees skyrocket.

If you broke life down into little day-by-day specifics, the list of injustices would be so long you'd have to cut down all the trees in the Brazilian rain forest just to make enough paper to record it. The good news, however, is that there is no record that Joshua and Caleb ever complained. Perhaps they had learned the secret of happiness—to accept the fair with the unfair.

There's even more good news. Forty years later when the rest of that ad hoc bunch was dead and buried, Joshua got himself appointed CEO and ram-rodded the takeover. And Caleb got the position of his choice in the new corporation.

Maybe there is some fairness after all.

7

Life Is Like a Roller Coaster, Except Faster

Some educators extol the benefits of driving simulators. Some praise computer projects. But for the sheer impact and clarity of the lesson to be taught, I can think of no learning machine more powerful than the roller coaster.

For the moment, forget the physics of how the thing works and consider the metaphorical paradigm of the ride itself.

You start slowly, comfortably seated, and you climb to the top, gradually and gently, so that you can take in the view—the sky in front and the huddled masses you have left behind. The higher you climb, the greater the glory and the more sense of power you have over the universe itself.

The apex is most spectacular of all. You seem to be at the summit, as high as any person has ever been before. The view and the thought of being on top of the world are breathtaking.

Then, just like that, you descend, but with a lot more velocity than when you came up. You are thrown back in the car so hard that you lose control of your thoughts. You try to scream for help, but you have forgotten the words. You fear for your life and doubt that there have ever been survivors.

About the time you think the ride is the worst it could ever be, it gets worse. You begin to climb, descend, and whirl all at the same time. For the next sixty seconds you are battered and banged and beaten every direction possible. At first you try to make adjustments—to anticipate and prepare for the next excruciating moment, but those moments come so rapidly that you find your movements behind the time, and this only makes matters worse.

So you resolve yourself to sure death, and you sit tense, waiting for the end. Just when you think you can take no more, and you make plans to abandon the ship regardless of the consequences, the machine slows and comes to a gentle stop.

Then you pay your money and do it all over again.

Now, for what daily event in life would you like to make this roller coaster ride an analogy?

Cleaning house? Making a sale? Raising a child? Taking a class in school? Cooking a meal for an important person? Driving to work? Going on a date? Aren't life's peaks and valleys, pauses and rushes wonderful!

8

Monday Today Is Better
Than Friday Someday

If they ever made a movie of human feelings, Impatience and Envy would look so much alike that the two roles would have to be played by the same actor. Sometimes I can't tell the difference.

There are people who wish they had someone else's property, and that's envy.

There are people who wish they were somewhere else, and that's impatience, particularly when they drive accordingly.

There are people who wish they were someone else, and that's dangerous.

But the group I don't understand are people who wish they were living in some other time. You hear them everyday.

"I dream of the time when I'll be eighteen and independent."

"Only five more years until retirement."

"I would give anything to be able to go back twenty years."

"How long until Friday?"

Now, are those the sighs of impatience or the cries

19

of envy? But I ask you—are there any sadder human utterances than those? Any greater pleas of futility and fantasy?

What's wrong with today, even if it's Monday?

If I wish into the future, I waste life. If I start Monday waiting for Friday, I have just blown away five days. If I count the years until retirement, I miss the joy the years before retirement promise.

On the other hand, if I wish for the past, I announce that I have wasted life. If I could retrace my steps twenty years, I wouldn't have the perspective, the wisdom, and the upper hand on life. And I wouldn't have the memories.

As I grow older, I have discovered that the past and the future are both fantasies. We've always known that about the past. We listen to people sigh and long for the "good old days," and we nod and smile and remember that the good old days weren't really as good as we remember them.

I catch myself thinking that if I could go back twenty years, I could play basketball again. The reality is, however, that I wasn't any Michael Jordan twenty years ago.

Living only for the future is just as much a fantasy. That Friday we wish for isn't real. It's only the product of our imaginations. If Friday turns out to be as exciting as we want it to be, we still have to make it that way. And that puts a lot of stress on Friday.

Why don't we instead just accept reality and make today exciting. At least we have today, and we may never get to the Friday of our fantasies.

When I took my shower today, the water rolled off my tummy and bounced on my feet making a neat pattern I've never seen before. Mary smiled at me at the breakfast table, and her eyes sparkled with a brilliance I had never seen before. Today I signaled, and the guy behind me slowed his car and let me change lanes. Today, the woman at the quick lunch place was friendly.

Today I had wonderful thoughts that I had never had before in my life. Today, someone explained the concept of the mole in chemistry to me, and although I still don't fully grasp it, I'm closer to understanding it than I have ever been before.

Today, I rested my hand against a chair, and I felt the pulse in my thumb—a proof of the life within me.

Today, I prayed, and God listened.

I'm glad it's today. I wouldn't want it to be any other time.

9

My Son Won't Follow in My Footsteps! His Feet Are Already Bigger Than Mine!

One day they are little with tiny hands and tiny feet wrapped in dainty booties. The next day they wrap their feet in size twelve brogans and fly off to Europe to consummate a business deal.

One day you caution them about playing in the street and eating sweets before supper. The next day they nag you because you eat eggs for breakfast and watch "Golden Girls" reruns on late night television.

One day you give them an extra quarter in the weekly allowance simply because they have been good. The next day they are busy putting together a portfolio of investments that would finance a bridge across the Pacific for people who don't like to fly.

Yes, children grow into adults. Innocent, dependent little things that coo and burble because you tickle their cheeks become important business persons with careers, goals, purposes, and briefcases. Helping children become self-sufficient, resourceful adults is the goal of parenthood. But I didn't think it would happen so fast.

I think I must have missed a stage in life. I remember a time not so long ago when I was a boy, and everywhere I went I was identified as the son of a successful man.

I dreamed then of a time when someone would be my son and would walk around with that identity.

But that time never came. Now I am known as a successful man's father.

And it happened so quickly.

10

Roses Have Thorns, But Americans Have Automobiles

Every living thing seems to have some sense of territory, some idea of the space that belongs to it by natural right.

The *National Geographic, Disney Channel Magazine,* and lesser biology books are filled with tales of how certain critters mark their territory and protect it.

Once I wanted to dust my rosebush. The bugs were beginning to creep on it, and I was concerned. When I got close enough to inspect my work, I violated the principle of territory, and a rosebush thorn "bit" me right on the end of my nose.

An old hen hatched chickens in her nest, and I

went out to assist. But I violated the principle of territory, and that old hen almost flogged me to death before I could get away.

I was walking through a pasture when I stopped to admire a big red bull with horns. As I stood appreciating the bull's strength, I violated the principle of territory, and the bull escorted me to the gate.

It seems to me that as a species, the American human animal senses a need for a little more personal territory than most other beasts on earth. You don't really pick that up while you are in America, but it becomes quite obvious when you travel internationally as an American.

In every country I have been in outside the United States and Canada, there is always somebody in my territory. When I ride the bus, there is at least one and sometimes as many as five in my territory. When I walk down the street, there are people in front and behind—close enough to be in my territory. When I go to a restaurant, there is somebody in my territory watching me eat.

Because Americans seem to have a need for more territory, they have adapted to their habitat the use of the automobile. If you asked any patriotic person the purpose of the automobile, he or she would say it was designed to get you anywhere fast. But everytime I drive in the city at 4:00 P.M. and watch bicycles and pedestrians moving faster than I am, I realize that that notion is one of the great American myths.

The true purpose of the American automobile, and the one that directs its design and function, is to designate territory.

In these years of concern about fuel and ozone, I hear talk of a bicycle revolution—of a time when Americans will pedal across the distances that separate them from friends and work places.

I have been to bicycle societies such as China, and I don't think it's going to happen here.

Riding a bicycle is more than a mode of travel. It is a shared personal experience.

We Americans need more space than that.

I Would Rather Be Reading

You've seen all those bumper stickers and T-shirts extolling someone's favorite fantasy and escape hatch.

"I Would Rather Be Flying."

"I Would Rather Be Surfing."

"I Would Rather Be Jogging."

"I Would Rather Be Skydiving."

"I Would Rather Be Doing Anything That Endangers Life And Limb."

Well, at my age speed and risk are not the thrills they once were. No longer do I see any particular need to drive the car really fast through a narrow alley or to ride in a barrel down a big hill or to eat goldfish while crowded in a phone booth.

For me, thrill and fun have become the by-products of serenity. For the sheer excitement of it all, for the stimulation of the pulse and tensing of hair follicles, is there any activity in all the world more thrilling than to wake up in a warm bed on a cold morning, reach over and grab a favorite tome, without so much as wrinkling the cover, don the bifocals, and spend the next three hours reading about somebody else rushing the rapids and chasing whales? Now, that's life.

Notice the maturity in the above scene. Not only do I not ask for activity, I have even grown past that time when I dreamed of doing my reading in some exotic place, like on the steps of the Louvre or on a deserted Caribbean isle.

Just my bed and a book—that's all the equipment I need for my escape. I don't even need an exotic book anymore. As the years go by, I am finding the joy and meaning I missed the first time through in the books of my childhood.

Now that I have lived long enough to have loved

the person of my choice for a while, *The Scarlet Letter* is no longer a simple story about a woman wearing a red letter. It is a myriad of emotions and thoughts that go beyond words and can only be expressed with grins and tears.

Now that I have lived long enough to have lost some of the fish I have hooked and have suffered my own kind of leg injuries, *Moby Dick* is no longer a simple tale of how whale boats smell. It is a diary too poignant for comfort.

Now that I have lived long enough that my own son has made his raft and floated down the river, *Huckleberry Finn* is more than a simple tale of someone growing up. It is a report of the transitions in life we all face.

Now that I have lived long enough to watch my three-year-old granddaughter develop rational skills, *Alice in Wonderland* is more than a simple story about a girl who falls in a hole. It is a wise exploration of sensibility and sanity.

That's the kind of emotional mountaintop I've climbed recently by just lying around in bed with a book.

As a window into the world of thrill and escape, reading beats most other activities because it is inexpensive and portable. Can you imagine jumping out of an airplane or skiing down a mountain without spending a small fortune?

There is, however, one small problem. Occasionally, you do have to stir a bit to find a new supply. Going to the bookstore or to the library can be such a frustrating project. Piles of books just lying around present no particular problem. But books in libraries and bookstores are neat and orderly with titles open and public, screaming out for your inspection. And inspection causes me to put everyone of them into one of three categories: 1) Books I have read but would love to read again. 2) Books I have never read but intend to before I die. 3) Books that make me feel guilty because I should have read them already.

That categorizing is what causes my frustration. I look at all those titles. I think of how long it takes me to read just one book. I compute how short life is. I think of all the books I will never read, and I get discouraged.

For me, there is one powerful antidote for such discouragement. I go home, jump into bed, pull the covers up, and reread a good book.

I like being too mature to need any other kind of thrill.

12

I'd Go for It, But I Don't Know Where It Is

The other evening I was running down the street. To the untrained eye, it might have looked as if I were jogging. The fact was that I had forgotten where I had left my car, and I was hurrying to find it before it got too dark to look.

Some fellow in a Blazer drove by, rolled down his window, and yelled, "Go for it, man. Go for it!"

Not long ago I was making a speech to a labor group. In midstream, I stopped the flow long enough for a little attention-getting gimmick and told a joke belittling management. It was a cheap trick, but it worked. Everybody giggled, and those who had dozed off woke back up in a fit of guilt. One lady yelled her endorsement, "Go for it, man. Go for it!"

The other Saturday I gathered a pillow and a blanket and went to the television room to keep my scheduled appointment with the game of the week. I was just completing warm-up rituals—taking off my socks, fluffing the pillow, and strategically locating the channel changer—when Mary came in. She watched my actions, ascertained my intent, nodded her approval, and said, "Go for it, man, Go for it!"

Now I have one question. Were all these people talking about the same place? Where exactly is "It"?

The problem with these encouragers is that they are never specific enough. There should be a federal law that requires such encouragement to come with directions.

I'm not afraid to set plans. I'm not even afraid to dream big dreams. And I'm definitely not afraid to use the energy and make the effort to get there. But I'm just not sure which direction is forward.

I don't admire track stars. I envy them. Their lot in life is easy. They know where the gold is. They line up where someone tells them to. They start on cue. They make all left-hand turns, and they stop when someone crosses a line. If they're the first to cross, they get the gold. Track events are simple. Life is tough.

Once I decided I wanted another college degree. Everybody said to go for it, so I did. But when somebody gave me that degree, I realized that wasn't It.

Once I decided to run a marathon. Everybody said to go for it, so I did. But when I finished the race in a state of complete euphoria, I still had the presence of mind to know that wasn't It.

Since I don't know where It is and can't find It, I have begun to work on another theory. Maybe It doesn't really exist. Maybe the real achievement is in the going and not in the getting there. Maybe those encouragers are just wordy. Rather than shouting "Go for it," they can clarify and simplify their message by just yelling, "Go!"

I Sweat, Therefore, I Am

A fellow named Descartes was having a serious identity crisis. Some people have identity crises but to a lesser degree. They worry about whether they are summer or winter personalities, whether they look best in bright colors or pastels. Some question events and ponder the meaning of life.

Descartes had it worse than that. He didn't even know if he existed. Perhaps he didn't have any teething children to keep him awake at night, or he didn't have a boss who mistook him for a horse instead of a human, or he didn't have in-laws who thought he could do better. Whatever the problem, he didn't know if he was real.

So he sat down and thought about it. History doesn't tell us where he sat to think, but for his sake, I hope it was by a creek bank under a cottonwood tree where sunbeams, streaking through its branches, were making patterns in the shade. Wherever he sat, he thought, and he thought, and he thought until he thought, "I think, therefore, I am."

Since I don't have the luxury of creek banks and cottonwood trees and time to think, I have to seek the proof of my existence in some other way. I have found such evidence in sweat.

For a simple, understandable symbol of reality sweat is more powerful than thought. It is, well, more real.

First, there is the issue of morality. Sweat is honest. We all know that. Thought is suspect. Can you imagine a TV commercial where some character with sincerity in his voice and a grandfatherly kindness in his face is saying emphatically, "In our company, we earn money the old-fashioned way. We think about it."

Or, when someone admires your new car, will you ever respond with that tone that bridges the gap between humility and sheer pride, "Thank you! I earned it by the thought inside my brow"?

Not in our society. We trust sweat, but we don't much believe in thought.

Besides that, sweat is easier to pick up with the senses than thought is. Do you remember that time when you and your favorite person were sitting in the porch swing listening to soft music playing in the background? The moon was big. The flowers smelled of spring and life. You moved closer and closer until you could feel each other breathe.

About then your favorite person broke the silence with a romantic plea, "A penny for your thoughts." Here was your chance to get rich, and you sat there dumbfounded because you weren't aware that you were thinking. You had no evidence of the existence of thought, no concrete proof.

Sweat is a different matter. When you sweat, you know it. You can taste yourself. You're out mowing the lawn on a hot July day. You've let the grass grow too long. The kids' toys lurk as half-buried hazards in the underbrush. The blade is dull, and the machine doesn't run all that well.

In the midst of all that you lick the corner of your mouth with a flick of the tongue, and immediately you know you exist. You can taste the evidence— salty and pleasant—concrete assurance of reality and life.

When you sweat, you can also smell yourself. After you've run about five miles farther than you meant to, don't you enjoy pulling your shirt off and whiffing up that fine aroma as it goes past your nose?

Deodorant manufacturers have spent millions of dollars trying to convince us that that isn't a very pleasant smell, and I suppose they're right. I don't much enjoy the smell of someone else's sweat, but I find some delight in my own at times.

Is there anytime when you're more aware of yourself, of your own reality and meaning, than when you have just completed a tough physical job, sweated through your pores and through your clothes, and are exuding a salty very human smell? At that moment, with the breath you have to gasp for, you just want to shout out, "I'm real."

Poor Descartes. For all that thinking, he missed the most obvious point and went about his pursuit backwards. Only if he woke up one morning and discovered he couldn't sweat, could he then doubt his existence.

Poor Penmanship Is a Natural Talent

My teacher once confused my writing of "not" for "now," and I failed the exam. My spouse hurried downtown to meet me when the note I had left on the refrigerator door had said that I was downstairs. I made notes at the business meeting, but three days later, I couldn't decode them, and I almost missed the deal.

I can summarize with an observation free of arrogance: "I don't write very well." Then I try to go on with life without any noticeable limitation from it.

But I'm not sure my poor penmanship is as cute as I once thought it was. I've been listening to myself and my peers lately, and I wonder if there might be hidden in our humoring a subtle message. We have become a people who don't put much stock in hand skills.

I collect old textbooks. I enjoy learning what the fifth graders learned in '06. But the most enjoyable parts of my old textbooks are the blank pages, front and back, where our great grandmothers and great grandfathers, when they were ten years old, wrote love notes to each other.

Those notes have taught me history and universality. The message of ten-year-olds is universal. Kids of every era make eyes and flirt, and whether you call it billing and cooing or something else, the activity is about the same.

On the other hand, the names are historical. I see such gems as, "Beulah loves Oscar," "Herman loves Bertha Sue," and I realize that the world does change in some ways.

The handwriting is a real eye opener. In every signature, in every margin notation, there is a flair, a distinctive quality of personal attention and a striving for clarity. Obviously, those people cared about how it looked, and somewhere in the educational process, they had trained their hands. I don't think you would ever hear them say rather nonchalantly, "I don't write very well."

I visited China and was overwhelmed at what I saw. Although their written language may be a little difficult to master, penmanship is still a valued art to be practiced by every literate person. They work at it, and they emphasize quality.

When you visit homes with young children, the proud parents don't bombard you with Little League trophies or have the child perform dance routines. They bring out the child's art and penmanship books for you to admire and comment on.

When you visit shrines to the Chinese greats, you don't visit homes of warriors. You visit the homes of scholars and artists, people who had the discipline to practice the craft of penmanship.

You may protest: "This is twentieth-century America. This is the Information Age. We need to develop our minds and our reasoning skills. We don't have time to waste on penmanship."

You may have a point. However, that kind of reasoning has a flaw. One of the greatest teachers I have ever met, a lady named Dixie, taught me the most important lesson of learning. "The hands feed the mind," and she showed me how by teaching a child to make a perfect 8.

From that demonstration I learned the deeper, more subtle lesson. Training the hands is training the mind.

Poor penmanship probably is a natural talent, but that doesn't mean we have to live with it.

15

Middle Age Is When All Problems Can Be Solved by Losing Weight and Flossing Your Teeth

The older we get the simpler life is.

A couple of months ago I damaged my knee. Now, I know about damaged knees. I'm a college football coach, and I see these young hulks with damaged knees about once a week. They hobble some, limp slightly, grimace during sprints and other unappealing practice times, and play out the rest of the season.

They then go into the hospital for major deconstruction where the specialists rebuild the legitimates, rewire the collaterals, correct the curvature, borrow the bones, and remove some cartridge. I don't understand all that language, but I know this is serious.

Those healthy young human colts then lie confined to their beds for weeks while coeds bring them the college version of Meals on Wheels until nourished enough to begin the grueling process of rehabilitation.

When I damaged my knee, the result was worse than any I had ever seen before. I didn't hobble through practice and grimace when I found the chore unpleasant. I lay writhing on the ground in agony, thinking that if I had been a horse, they would have shot me on the spot.

By mustering all the desire to live I could, I managed to make it home. Surely I, too, would become one of the growing crowd with zippers on the knee.

Through sheer determination and the discipline of mind over pain, I endured that long night before my doctor's appointment. My knee had taken on the appearance of a rotten cantaloupe, and I lay on the couch gritting my teeth while holding my leg up in the air trying to defuse the throbs that came with such force that the couch shook.

The next morning, still in agony, I went to see the

specialist, not so much to get a diagnosis but to see how much time I had to call in the family before the inevitable operation.

The doc came in, grinned at me, made small talk, poked around a bit, took one X ray, and said over his shoulder on his way out of the room, "Well, there isn't much here except a little bruise. Lose weight and floss your teeth. It ought to be all right in a few days."

And that was it.

I had a toothache not long ago. This wasn't one of those modern aches that bites back as a well-deserved punishment for chewing on ice. This was an old-fashioned toothache—the kind that starts at the tooth, numbs the jaw, runs down the arm, and ends up somewhere in the vicinity of your socks.

I went to see the dentist, a bright young fellow who used to play on our football team and should have understood pain.

He grinned a bit, made small talk, poked around some, and said over his shoulder on his way out of the room, "Well, there isn't much here except a little infection. Lose weight and floss your teeth. It ought to be all right in a few days."

And that was it.

I had a problem at work. For some unexplained reason my responsibilities began to increase until they had multiplied like houseflies on a humid night.

There were pests everywhere, and I was wearing myself out just swatting at them.

While my colleagues discussed last night's television fare, presented reviews of all the latest best sellers, and boasted about their weekend skiing trips, I iced down the bags under my eyes and watched my arms being stretched longer by carrying around a heavy briefcase.

Finally, I went to see my boss. He is a congenial man and reasonable. He would surely know something about suffering. He had worked his way through the ranks to his position. Without exaggeration or even the slightest hint of whine in my voice, I presented my problem.

He grinned at me, made small talk, and said to me over my shoulder as he ushered me out of his office. "Well, there isn't much here except a little disorganization and lack of control. Lose a little weight and floss your teeth, and it ought to be all right in a few days."

And that was it.

Even Mary got into the act. Surely she would be the one person who understands. After all, we've been married thirty-three years, and she has watched me grow better instead of older.

I walked in one evening and caught her with that special twinkle in her eye that communicates love, passion, and companionship. That same twinkle first attracted me to her. That was the twinkle that she looked at me with through her wedding veil. So, I thought I had found a willing ear and a tender heart.

I told her the whole story—in vivid detail—the sore knee, the sore tooth, the harried schedule, and the absence of appreciation for me in it all.

Mary didn't say a word, and when I had finished, she grinned at me, made small talk, and went back to writing names in our grandchild memory book. As she did she said, "You know, dear, if you would lose weight and floss your teeth, you would still be kind of attractive."

That's it. I'm through. I'm going to find a mountaintop somewhere in the Ouachita Mountains in Arkansas, and I am going into the guru business.

I will sit cross-legged day after day, look into the distance, and take on the appearance of wisdom.

If someone should ever climb that mountain and ask me any kind of question, no matter what, I am going to demand big dollars before I even utter a sound. If someone should happen to pay that sum, I will open my mouth and speak slowly and profoundly, "Lose weight and floss your teeth. That's the path to happiness."

16

I Journal with Tie Stains

Keeping a diary is a time-honored enterprise. There is much evidence that ancient Greek and Roman notables on regular occasions sat down with quill in hand and chronicled the events of the day.

One seventeenth-century English chap named Pepys worked so diligently on his daily record that the volume is still considered great literature, serving two worthwhile purposes. Scholars stay awake late into the night and debate how much of it is accurate, and high school students stay awake late into the night trying to decide how to pronounce this guy's name for the next day's class.

Thoreau kept a diary. Anne Frank did too.

Even in this postmodern era, people are still keeping diaries. Of course, to keep up with the times, we have given the activity a computer-age name. We now call it "journaling." (That's how we keep up to date and ready for the twenty-first century. We take nouns and use them as verbs to describe something that folks have been doing for twenty-five hundred years.)

Obviously, not all these modern-day journals will make it into the realm of long-lasting literature. That's not important. Rather, it's the activity of journaling that's significant. As its promoters tell me, journaling is the process of tracing your pilgrimage through life and keeping a record of the high and low points.

They convinced me. I decided that I did need some kind of an account of my pilgrimage, but the overall tone of my journaling should reflect a common theme. That's when I came to grips with my two most outstanding characteristics. 1) All the big events in my life center around food. 2) I'm a sloppy eater.

I put those two together and came up with the proper vehicle for the literature of my life's pilgrimage. I journal with tie stains. If you consider the advantages, perhaps you too could start such a diary.

For one thing, the memories are more active. When you read words in a journal two years after the fact, you may or may not have any recollection of the emotions. But every morning when I look into the mirror to put the finishing touches on a double windsor, I spot the gravy stain on my tie, and my taste buds recall the pot roast. My nose remembers the cabbage boiling and fresh bread rising, and all the other taste sensations come rushing back.

The reason is obvious enough. When I record with

tie stains, the literary style is completely natural. There isn't anything contrived or strained or artificial. I'm good at this genre.

Of course, I know that these ties aren't going to last forever. Four centuries from now high school students won't have to miss sleep trying to remember how to pronounce my name.

The real reason I champion the tie-stain journal is utilitarian; when the seven-year famine comes, I'll just get out my journals, boil them to make broth, and have enough nourishment to make it through the duration.

17

My Son and My Money Attend the University of Hard Knocks

A famous psychologist pointed out the perils of modern parenthood rather succinctly: "We are so busy giving our children what we never had that we forget to give them what we did have."

I remember the gifts my father gave me—baseball gloves, a guitar, a bridle for my horse, a new typewriter—but of all those, two are the most precious. My father gave me the gift of knowing the value of honesty and the joy of work.

I suppose I could wish for other kinds of property in the legacy—a new set of wheels, a condo on the sea, an interest-bearing account large enough to take care of most normal needs.

Those things, however, are temporary. Cars wear out, condos get battered by hurricanes, and bank accounts wither from abuse. On the other hand, those most precious gifts my father spent his years amassing for me and passing down are lifelong. Regardless of the economic trends or world situations, I shall always have them, and so long as I do, they shall serve me by making life richer and more rewarding. That's the greatest kind of inheritance of all.

Oh! How I need to remind myself of how much my children need these very same gifts from me!

How often I need to remind myself that the best education in the country is still offered at the University of Hard Knocks, and I must be prepared to encourage my children's enrollment and even help pay the tuition.

Notice how simple and easy it all sounds. But it isn't. This may reasonably be one of the hardest, most humbling, and most tiring missions of my whole life. Although I understand all the virtues of such an education, I am not sure I can bear the pain of having my children attend that academy.

Let's look at just one aspect as an example, namely, separation. Is there anywhere a parent who does not have the continuous dread of having at least one child come and say, "Well, I have just been accepted and given full scholarship to the finest university anywhere, but of course it is on the other side of the country."

Let me warn you. When that point in life comes, you just have to know that you're in for some separation—four years, six years, ten years—depending on how much graduate school is involved. And despite your stiff upper lip and your pseudo-smile, you know that separation is going to cause you a little pain along the way.

That kind of pain from that kind of separation is a cakewalk compared to the pain that can come from the separation of having a child at the University of Hard Knocks. That first university requires a separation in distance, but that second university might require a separation of emotions. And that can be almost unbearable.

Another problem with the University of Hard Knocks is that this is one school that requires special parental support. With a child there, we may have to say one or all of the following:

"You're the one who left your toys at Grandma's house. Now you'll just have to learn to live without them for a while."

"You're the one who put off writing the paper until the night before it's due. Now you'll just have to stay up by yourself and do it."

"You're the one who got picked up for speeding and drove the insurance rates through the sunroof. Now you'll just have to manage to pay the bill or learn the skill of walking."

"You're the one who wanted to move out and live in your own apartment. Now you'll just have to learn to live without meat for these three days until you get paid."

Those are hard lessons offered by the University of Hard Knocks. They are hard on the students, and they play havoc with the emotions of the parents as well.

The whole problem is trying to discover the operational meaning of love. One moment I say to myself, "I love my son too much to let him endure this." The next moment I say to myself, "I love my son too much to deprive him of learning the lessons of life."

It's a personal conflict between two feelings that live within us, and it isn't easily negotiated. That conflict reminds me that love has a tough side too.

18

You Never Know the Worth of a Toe Until You Break It

One nice result of going on a diet, particularly when you are successful, is that you get reacquainted with body parts you haven't had close contact with for years.

I went on a diet, lost a little weight, and rediscovered the joy of knowing my feet. I like my feet. Through the years they have carried me through some difficult spots and fun experiences. They work hard and don't grumble all that much.

I especially have become emotionally linked with the little toe on my right foot. He's a strange-looking chap, built like me, short and round. I can't really tell that he does all that much. He just hangs around the crowd and follows along when the body decides to go somewhere—never making many decisions, never carrying too much responsibility. He just is.

The reason I am attracted to this fellow is not sympathy but identity. I see myself as the little toe on the collective body of humankind. That's why I enjoy sitting and watching my little toe. That's why I don't mind waiting half-naked in the doctor's office for an hour and twelve minutes for a five-minute diagnosis and prescription. I turn those precious times into significant educational endeavors in which I learn about human service and the purpose of life in the grand scheme of things. I study the little toe on my right foot.

A couple of months ago, my perspective changed, and I learned a powerful lesson about little toes—real and metaphorical.

I was drying myself after a shower and a nosy wasp flew through an open window and began to pester me. With my body dripping and my hands full of towel, I took what at the time seemed to be a normal course of action. I kicked at the beast.

In retrospect, I see my foolishness. It was really a stupid stunt—something that some psychologists would call an "animal instinct." I know of no animal except the human animal dumb enough to kick at a wasp with a bare and vulnerable foot.

Fortunately, I missed the wasp, but I didn't miss the wall. At the point of impact several members of my anatomy complained, but none cried out as sharply as the little toe on my right foot. This fellow was in acute pain. After trying the therapeutic value of dancing around on one foot and blowing in that general direction, I finally calmed down enough to inspect the damage. Even without any Hippocratic training, I could tell there was a problem. The little fellow was no longer just short and round. He now had an ugly hump in the middle of his back, and he was turning blue.

At the hospital emergency room the highly trained and caring staff confirmed my diagnosis. "You broke your little toe," they told me in a tone that seemed to have just a touch of repressed laughter. Then they put a piece of tape on it, gave me some pain pills, and sent me home, probably so they could properly catalog my story in their collected anthology of the dumb things they have seen during their careers.

That night, after taking pain pills and gulping big glasses of water, I went to bed and fell into a fitful semisleep. It wasn't long until the pain pills and the water took charge of my personal schedule, and I found it necessary to get out of bed and go to the bathroom, not once but often. At that point the little toe on my right foot developed the personality of a one-year-old who has just been told to eat his vegetables. The toe pouted, cried, whimpered, and refused to do his part. Until that very moment, I have never realized how much work the little toe really does do when it comes time for a body to get out of bed.

I asked other body parts to take up the slack, but soon they started complaining. First, my stomach muscles growled because of the new work assignment, and my forearms got sore. With all those body parts angrily protesting any movement at all, I tried putting off the urge as long as I could, and my kidneys got out of sorts over the delay. Then my brain started reacting to all the conflict, and I had one of the most miserable nights of my life, all because the little toe on my right foot was hurting.

The next day, well-meaning friends said to me, "Wow, you look terrible!"

"Yes," I explained, "I had a miserable night. I'm injured."

"Where?" they asked, as if they had sympathy to offer.

"The little toe on my right foot," I answered, and they, at least the kind ones, turned their backs so that they wouldn't snicker in my face.

When it was all over, I found great encouragement in the whole ordeal. There is a purpose for every one of us, even if we are just a little toe.

Our Children Are the Story Problems of Adulthood

Do you remember those story problems from elementary school math classes?

You never had enough facts. You always had to read between the lines. You had to put together a formula for action that demanded assumptions and risks. You used all your mental powers and that wasn't enough. You learned by trial and error and never had any way of knowing whether you got it right. You always had a headache from all the work.

Can you think of anything that describes parenthood any better than that?

Do you remember those school days when you got so frustrated with that endless barrage of story problems that you finally got enough courage to speak your mind. You held up your hand, waited your turn, and asked with a tone somewhere between sincere and sarcastic, "Why do we have to do this? How is this ever going to help us in life?"

Your math teacher, a young man all dressed up with a tie too short and a plastic liner in his shirt pocket, grimaced, scowled, furrowed his brow, and finally said in a tone too weak to be persuasive, "It'll make your brain grow."

All these years, you have had to live with that weak excuse for doing all that math, and on top of that you have the nagging suspicion that maybe your brain is oversized.

Now that I have achieved the station of parent, I have discovered the real reason for story problems. In a small way, they begin to prepare us for what's ahead.

Let's consider some current homework assignments.

1. The two-month-old that sleeps all day and cries all night. The fourteen-year-old that sleeps all day and cries all night.

2. The fourteen-year-old who can't remember that he is supposed to take the trash out on Tuesday but knows the daily batting averages of every player in the major leagues.

3. Any kid agile enough to skateboard but too clumsy to wash dishes.

4. The junior-higher who changes complete life-time friendships every hour on the hour.

5. The child who voluntarily comes up and kisses you while you are rebuking her for misdemeanors.

6. The child who didn't have to use the bathroom when you first started on the trip but needs to fifteen minutes later.

7. The child who thinks your tastes run to neo-Neanderthal and your outfits are dorky, but still wears your clothes.

From all our experiences in school, we may not have any better idea of how to go about finding the solutions to the problems of parenthood, but at least we have had some foretaste of the frustration associated with the office.

There is one positive note. We should at least be a little wiser than our own math teacher was. Some of these nights our own little story problems will come barging into the family room, calculators in hand and worry on the face, and interrupt our reading, television watching, and soda sipping with that old familiar cry, "Why do we have to do this stuff anyway? We are never going to use this in life."

At that point, we can get a look on our face that's somewhere between a grin and a sneer, and we can say with the satisfaction of knowing, "Because some day, my dear, you may be the parent of my grandchildren." And we can go back to sipping our soda.

20

Watch for Rising Rock

I wish to announce my new profession. I am now an official road sign critic.

I thought about being a drama critic, but I could not master the art of reading the playbill after they turn the house lights off. I thought about being a movie critic; but every time I go to the theater, my shoes stick to the floor, and I can't get my legs to work.

That's why I have chosen to be a road sign critic. It involves a little travel, which is always exciting, and it does put me into the mainstream of American culture. I am convinced that when we record the mores and customs of contemporary life, we must include our road signs as representative pieces of art work and literature.

I personally enjoy those signs that carry gentle nudges and work at several levels. Just standing on a street corner and reading the sheer poetry that reminds me to "Walk with light" makes my day. As the sign suggests, life is a matter of choice. We could spend our days walking in darkness, but how much more pleasant it is when we "Walk with light." I am refreshed by the imagery.

I also appreciate literature that is straightforward and to the point. For just the brilliance of simplicity in writing, there is no better example than the sign that tells us, "Obey your signal." But in this genre of road signs a tour de force is the strong, unmistakable statement, "Do Not Enter."

On the other hand, I sometimes enjoy those signs that have an intricate plot. "No right turn on red after stop" weaves its multiactions and conflicts together so masterfully that you are amazed of how it all works out in the end.

Sometimes plot structure can be overdone. "No right turn on school days between 8 and 4 when children are present" is a good example of how a story line gets bogged down with too much detail and loses the reader's interest.

My all-time favorites are those road signs that communicate through the art of satire. These are classics. Not only do they bite a bit, but they point out the problem of futility.

Imagine for a moment that you have just topped the crest of a big hill. Below you is a sharp decline, hairpin curves, one thousand foot cliffs, and road construction. At this point consider the impact of these words: "Proceed with caution" and try to come up with any other options.

Another fascinating example of this kind of look at futility is the now classic, "Loose gravel ahead! Protect your windshield." Is there any more succinct statement of the human condition than this? You may be acutely aware of danger, but there is no possible strategy for coping. You could put your whole car in a giant paper bag and seal the top with a plastic tie. You could drive backwards. You could ask a passenger to lie across the hood as a human shield. Or, you could just turn around and go home. Such a sign is great satire. It leaves the reader wallowing in a bog of irony.

That brings us to my four-thumbs-up choice for the best of all road signs, full of drama and irony, panic and humor. You will find it always in a beautiful spot, high up in a mountain pass where the air is thin and the view spectacular.

As you drive along in awe of the wonders of nature

and the human ability to build roads in incredible places, there, when you are least expecting it, is the gem of all road signs. "Watch for falling rock."

When I first encountered this piece of work, I took it as a serious warning of possible danger. I soon saw the fallacy of that thought. Suppose a rock did fall just as you were driving by. The only value the warning would provide is that you would know what killed you.

More recently, I have begun to appreciate that sign with a different perspective. Rather than a warning at all, it is a sign with tour guide functions. If a rock should happen to fall, the sight would surely be spectacular—one you wouldn't want to miss especially with a good chance of death impending.

With that in mind, I submit my original road sign manuscript: "Watch for rising rock." Since rocks don't usually rise, we don't really need the warning. But if a rock ever did rise on a mountain pass, it would indeed be sad if all the drivers missed it.

21

Tonto Is the Real Hero Because He Kept the Secret

Can you imagine Tonto on the talk show circuit?

Oprah would advertise, "People with a deep secret they are just dying to tell should tune in for tomorrow's show!"

Geraldo, clutching the microphone and pacing nervously, would listen to Tonto's tale, and then he would ask, "Tell us, Tonto, where do you two really go when you go riding off into the sunset?"

Donahue would have some psychologist on hand to analyze this fellow, explaining the potential mental danger of living life with suppressed knowledge.

Soon the tabloids would pick up the story and blare the headlines in the checkout stations so bright that the milk would curdle in the grocery carts.

FAMOUS COWBOY WEARS MASK TO HIDE LIFE THREATENING ZITS!

FAITHFUL COMPANION TELLS ALL!

With this kind of publicity, it wouldn't be long until Tonto would be about the hottest interview around, and some author would finally compile what we have all been waiting for: the unauthorized biography of the Lone Ranger—another hero with clay feet.

The good news is that Tonto will never tell. He just isn't that kind of guy, and that's why he's a hero.

I admire the Lone Ranger for everything he has accomplished. He saved the ranch, rescued the maiden, intercepted the bad guys, got the mail through, and didn't even send a bill.

I also admire Tonto for being brave enough to know when to keep his mouth shut.

In this age of Verbal Indecent Exposure, that's a refreshing trait. Everywhere one turns these days, there is somebody in the name of candor telling it all, and if they don't know anything shocking about somebody else, they tell it about themselves.

My ears are too tender for too much candor. The rest of my anatomy seems to take it in stride, but when the conversation gets too personal, and the dirty linen gets too close, my ears turn red.

Through the talk shows, newspapers, and unauthorized biographies, I find myself learning more about people than I really wanted to know.

Do you have any idea what my biggest problem is? Well, you can keep on wondering. I am not going to tell you. It's not only personal, it's private.

Remember, Tonto is my hero.

22

I Love Youth—It's Teenagers I Don't Understand

Youth is the May of life, so tender and gentle, so creative and curious, so full of energy and enthusiasm, so full of the sap of happiness, so eager and ready.

Youth is a time of hormones and poetry. A time of distant memories.

Youth is a time of active senses and an open-mouthed awe of life. It is changing moods and constantly changing dreams and plans.

Youth is a time of expectancy.

Youth is geometry class the day it all fit together, and we understood. It is long summer days and December nights underneath a sky glittering with stars.

Youth is milk shakes poured from metal cans with two straws. It's jelly beans and second helpings, with little concern for calories.

Youth is the carefree and confident agreement to accept the burden of making the world a better place.

In this youth is the wonder of hope, the direction of the future.

So, why do we waste this time of life on people

whose total vocabulary consists of "Soooo?" "That's not fair," and "You don't trust me."

Why do we waste it on people with Walkmans growing out of their shoulders and noise blaring in one ear and out the other loud enough to awaken half the population of Sao Paulo?

Why do we waste youth on people who think that it is a human rights infraction to keep a path through the clutter in their room, to make their beds at least once a month, and to carry their own dirty dishes to the sink?

Why do we waste it on people whose intellectual curiosity leads to the depth of such questions as, "Is this going to be on the test?" and "Why do we have to learn this anyway?"

Why do we waste it on people who one minute say, "Do you mind? I want to do this by myself," and the next minute say, "Could I have some help with this? What do you expect from me?"

Don't get me wrong. I rather like these people. I find them refreshingly honest and often amusing. But I'm disturbed that they don't appreciate what they have.

I have a better idea. Let's make it a law that the only people who can be carefree and curious and confident about the future are those old enough to have once held a definite opinion about whether Truman should have fired MacArthur.

Let's make it a law that the only people who can stay out late at night and still get up early the next day are those who own 78 rpm records.

Let's make it a law that the only people who can live on a diet that consists only of spicy pizza and sugared cola and still not gain weight are those whose image of Elizabeth Taylor comes from memories of *National Velvet*.

Let's make it a law that the teenagers should be as concerned about the middle-aged as the middle-aged are concerned about teenagers. Let's make them shake their heads and ask of no one in particular, "What's wrong with those crazy middle-aged these days?"

Let's make them worry so much that they are driven for help to books with such titles as:

How to Help Your Parents Survive and Thrive

The Strong-willed Coot

How to Really Love Your Grandpa

Everything I Need to Know I Learned in a Korean Foxhole

Thinking about youth this way has some value. It reminds us that youth is not a matter of the number of candles on a birthday cake but rather a frame of mind—for now and for the rest of our lives.

23

I Act This Way Because
I've Been Watching You

Children copy role models, but adults play One-upmanship. Actually, the games are about the same, but the adult version is a little more sophisticated.

The children pick their role models, observe them closely, and try to imitate them as precisely as possible.

The adults don't always pick the best models; but they observe closely, and then they try to imitate but with just a little extra movement in the maneuver. That's the game of One-upmanship.

Having grown out of the children's version and playing the adult game for several years, I have finally begun to discern some of the finer points of play, some of the techniques—well within the rules— to help insure victory.

In respect to fair play, I offer the following list of tips free of charge. I call it "Nine Don'ts I Learned by Watching You."

1. *Don't reason with unreasonable people.*

Regardless of what your high school algebra teacher told you when she tried to give you a reason for doing that homework, logic can't stand up against an emotional appeal. You could decide to be unreasonable yourself, but that only produces two unreasonable people, and that's a stalemate at best.

The better plan is to calm the unreasonable into the reasonable, and the quickest way to do that is by being agreeable.

When your offspring, now a sobbing, screaming, adolescent, shouts at you, calmly say, "Yes, dear, you're absolutely right. I am the worst parent in the whole world, and I don't trust you."

When your student comes in, slams the door, glares, and proceeds to protest the grade you have given, gently respond, "You actually earned something three points better, but I gave you that grade because I don't like you."

2. *Don't do business with anyone who doesn't trust you.*

I especially worry about those people who are quite creative in imagining ways that I could cheat them. What are they going to do with all those thoughts once they have thought them up?

3. *Don't brag about your children when you're with people who have children the same age.*

This is just common sense. By the ancient laws of territorial rights I am required to prove to you that I am a better parent than you are, and the only proof is that my children are brighter, prettier, more polite, more obedient, and have had more severe children's diseases than yours have had. If you must brag about your children, make friends with a post.

4. *Don't show your home movies to people who are saving up to buy a Minicam.*

Reciprocity is the most vicious form of retaliation.

5. *Don't hold a grudge against someone who has already forgiven you.*

Not only does it weigh you down needlessly, it gives the other person the upper hand in future arguments.

6. *Don't try to bargain in a business deal with a man who wears a calculator on his belt.*

I don't distrust all people with calculators, but according to the historical principles of machohood, anything strapped to the waist can be used as a weapon.

7. *Don't play cards with anybody who wears a visor and a rubber thumb.*

Before entering any contest, look for the telltale signs that your opponent might be a pro. Not only will you lose in such an event, but you may even be in danger of losing your amateur status just by entering the fray. The revised version of this: Don't play pool with anybody who loops his or her forefinger around the stick.

8. *Don't ever let your children meet your old buddies from your school days.*

Credibility is covered by such a thin veil anyway. There is no reason to take chances.

9. *Don't ever reveal your complete list of don'ts.*

This advice is so subtle that it has taken me years to master. I used to travel great distances to conferences where my opponents, such as coaches and business competitors, were presenting the keynote address. I listened intently and took notes profusely. I thought I would learn what they knew, and then I would be as smart as they were. What I never learned until years later is that they always omitted the most vital point.

The revised version of this is: Don't trade recipes with anyone who enters chili-cooking contests.

24

Snakes and Robins Have Different Songs and Perspectives

Have you ever seen a happy snake? Even the harmless ones seem to have a sour disposition.

Can you blame them? Have you ever thought about what they have to travel through just to get where they want to be? They have to crawl through the muck and mire. Pebbles look like boulders. Their tummies are always covered with slime or grit. They can't ever really see where they're going past the next turn, and they eat live animals.

Have you ever seen an unhappy robin? They are about the most cheerful of all beasts. They wake up early just to sing. They dart and flit about as if life is just one giant joy.

Can you blame them? Have you ever thought about where they travel? They fly around in the tops of trees and among the honeysuckle blossoms. From their lofty perches, they look down on all other creatures. If they don't like the view, they just fly around until they find one that pleases them.

I don't understand enough about biology to enter into the study of the psychology of animal life, but it just seems to me that there is a logical reason for assigning those differences in "personality" types to snakes and robins.

If we ever wake up some morning, look in the mirror, and realize that we don't like the attitude on our face—if we stop and listen and realize that we aren't singing enough or don't enjoy the songs we are singing—maybe we ought to change perspectives. It wouldn't be as hard for us as it would for snakes.

The other day I was having lunch in an out-of-town restaurant when a middle-aged man and his early adolescent son came in. I didn't mean to stare or eavesdrop, but they were having so much fun together that I couldn't help myself.

Another man came in, saw the father and son, and with a startled look recognized the father. "What happened to you?" the newcomer asked. "You must have lost a hundred pounds."

"I have," answered the happy man.

"But how?" was the logical question, and everyone in the restaurant eavesdropped for the magic formula.

"I got a grip on it," answered Mr. Happiness.

"What? You got a grip on your diet?"

"I got a grip on life," the man answered, as he and his son beamed, "on all of life—diet, drinking, fatherhood, priorities, and even liking other people."

At that point I couldn't help myself. I turned and stared. I found it refreshing to come face-to-face with a happy man, a man who had a robin's perspective on life.

25

Samson Could Have Bought a Wig

I had to travel to California to give a speech. There were about one thousand people in the audience, and I was frightened. But the emcee introduced me by telling the crowd of my credentials. I had been a guest on their favorite radio program, and I knew the host personally. With that piece of information, the people "oohed" and "ahhed." I spoke, they listened, and I enjoyed the power of holding their attention.

I had to travel to New England to give a speech. There were about five hundred people in the audience, and I was frightened. But the emcee introduced me by telling the crowd of my credentials. I had written an article for their favorite magazine, and I knew the editor personally. With that piece of information, the people "oohed" and "ahhed." I spoke, they listened, and I enjoyed the power of holding their attention.

I had to travel to Africa to give a speech. There were about two hundred people in the audience, and I was frightened. But the emcee introduced me by telling the crowd of my credentials. I was teaching at one of their favorite colleges, and I knew the president personally. With that piece of information, the people "oohed" and "ahhed." I spoke, they listened, and I enjoyed the power of holding their attention.

After that I traveled to the Southwest and volunteered to speak at a little country church that sat on the edge of a cotton field at the end of a red dirt country road. There were about thirty people in the audience, and I was calm. The emcee introduced me by telling the crowd of my credentials. He said, "I don't know this man. I don't know where he lives or what he does, but he's here to speak to us this morning." With that piece of information, he sat down. Nobody "oohed" and "ahhed." Where was the rest of my introduction—that little gem that would impress those people so that I could speak with power?

All the while, as I pondered what to say, I felt like Samson. That man who introduced me had cut my hair off. Then I realized the awful truth. He didn't cut my hair. He had stolen my wig.

How often we tell ourselves that we are important people, that we have power. To impress people with that point, we cite our credentials.

Our power, our real power, however, is not to be found in our credentials. Our credentials are not what we are but what others think of us. Credentials are only a wig. Our credentials are not what we are inside but what we wear to impress others, and that's not enough to whip the Philistines when the crunch comes.

Those people who admire the wig don't know the person's anxieties when driving on a lonely road late at night. They don't know the person's hopes and fears while lying in bed after the lights are out.

That's the real person—the one without a wig.

Our credentials are what others give us, but true power is what God gives us.

Let me say that a different way. Our power is what we allow God to give us. If we are aware of that, we won't need the wig.

26

Computers Can't Cuddle

Like most families, we have a special day that we pause to celebrate each year. Unlike other families, it isn't a wedding anniversary, the birthday of a child, the day we moved into our house, or the day we were picked as an average family by a national television show.

At our house, we celebrate Bringing Home The Computer Day.

It was my idea. The kids had schoolwork to do. Mary had bills to pay. And I had important work. After all, we're living in the modern age. Simple little laborsaving devices should be in every home.

When I announced my decision, the kids cheered, and Mary trembled. "I'm not sure I could ever catch on," she pleaded.

I calmed her. I had an hour off the next day that I could devote to purchasing a machine and learning how to operate it. I would come home and teach everybody all I knew. It would be a simple procedure.

The next day I drove to the computer store, walked in, and sensed immediately that I was in deep trouble. The place gave me the creeps. The salesman came, with teeth shining and necktie blazing. He went straight into his spiel.

"Hello, there. I see you're admiring this little honey. Well, I don't blame you. You've got good taste. That little baby is our special XKG model. It has five hundred amps, fifty watts, and it bites megas. It comes with a built-in papier-mâché cutter, tweeters, rooters, amplifiers, gadgets, and progressive terminal anode posts. You can get the stripped-down model for a thousand dollars, or with a printer, software package, spreadsheet, tear sheet, bed sheet, and leather carrying case by just adding a million dollars to your purchase price. And it's all IBM compatible!"

I went into that store an intelligent, literate adult. I came out a frightened child.

Computer salespeople are worse than car salespeople. For one thing, they talk faster, and they don't use a single word of English. At least car sales personnel drop in a word I understand once in a while.

Computer salespeople are even worse than teachers, and those people haven't used ordinary English in a parent conference since McGuffey quit writing textbooks.

Out of fear of seeming monolingual, I bought the thing while I still had some sanity, and I took it home.

In full charge of all faculties, I ordered everybody out of the computer room and started the process of assembly. First, I worked on the desk—a simple wooden construction with three sides and four legs and four hundred other parts that didn't belong anywhere. After an hour or so of trying futilely to make everything fit and give a home to all those little parts, I broke down and committed the greatest breach of the macho code. I started to read the directions.

More dismay. Those instructions weren't just printed in non-English. They consisted of words and symbols from every conceivable phonetic system on earth. Nothing made sense. After putting legs where sides should go and screws where bolts should go, I surrendered completely. I called Mary.

She came with a calming smile and lent moral support. At first, she read the directions while I worked the assembly line. That was a nice system, and it should have worked, but it didn't. She began to read the directions in the language they were printed in. I became flustered with her. She became flustered with me. She started reading and pointing. Then she started pointing and screaming. Finally, when I had not one ounce of human dignity left, I stalked out of the room to go to the kitchen for reinforcement—a chocolate chip cookie. I deliberately munched slowly, and when I returned to the scene of the chaos, Mary had the whole mess looking something like a desk.

For a while, I sat on the chair I had bought for the occasion and watched her continue the task at hand. I soon grew tired of it all, and I went back to our bedroom and spent the day reading George Orwell's *1984.*

Once in a while, Mary would come in and give me a report. The desk was up and the computer was out. She finished programming the disks, and she found the escape button. She had just mastered the software and fed the mouse. Then she entered all the bills for the past three years, had a complete printout of our financial statement and economic forecasts. She had just finished writing letters to every known relative and was attaching the computer printout labels to envelopes.

I kept on reading that tale of a society that had lost its soul.

Each time Mary came, I noticed a change in her countenance. At first she was fearful. On subsequent visits, the fear disappeared, and she became confident. As the day wore on the confidence grew into exhilaration. And the exhilaration grew into power.

I grew afraid of her. About midnight I went into the computer room to ask her to come to bed. I never got her attention. She was huddled over that mass of beige plastic, staring intently, punching buttons, and grinning like Dr. Jekyll.

So, I went to bed alone and cried myself to sleep.

Sometime during the wee hours of the morning, she found her way to bed. I awoke from a fitful sleep but lay quietly so she would not know my anguish.

She slid over near me and accidentally touched me with her feet, her ice cold feet. I took my two toasty ones and wrapped them around hers.

She said, quietly and sincerely, "Thank you, dear," and she went to sleep.

I went to sleep, too, soon after that, knowing that I had a clear understanding of the difference between people and computers.

27

Crow Stew Is High in Cholesterol

Sometimes my mouth works as an independent agent and in no way represents the rest of the organs to which it is attached.

In other words, it talks crow. It's the mouth that does it. I don't know where it gets some of those opinions, observations, and predictions, but they just come flying out without any consideration for the consequences.

That's what I call talking crow, speaking before considering all the possibilities. When that happens, the world takes that crow, cooks it into a foul stew, and feeds it back.

The mouth brags about the children, then the children won't be cute on command.

The mouth extols the prowess of the favorite team, then when the battle begins the favorite team plays like Goliath, falling dead after the first flip of the slingshot.

The mouth promises that the job will be done by Saturday, but the people delivering the part needed to complete the job get lost and don't arrive until Sunday.

The mouth promises the mate a quiet evening at home alone, and fourteen old buddies show up to help cheer you through the evening.

Regardless of how it's served, crow stew tastes the same, and someday medical research will surely show that eating it is the number one cause of hypertension.

It's that mouth running too free that causes all the problems.

28

Garbage
Is Heavy

In my younger days when my profession as a coach was on the move, so were we. In fact, there was a period when our family of five changed houses about once a year.

In some ways, that's not as bad as it sounds. At least, such a routine helps you remember what it is you do own, and it helps you make some decisions about the importance of each possession.

Somewhere in all that process, somebody gave us a case of homemade pickles. History has dimmed the memory of the exact origin of these pickles and has caused something of a minor family debate.

As I remember it, some grateful parent gave us the pickles as a reward to me for outstanding teaching and service beyond the greatest expectations. In her old age, Mary falsely recalls that the next door neighbor gave them to us one day while he was cleaning out his garage.

Nevertheless, they were delightful-looking specimens—plump and green—and became one of our prized possessions.

Maybe because they looked so good or maybe because we just weren't ever hungry for pickles, we never opened the case. We just moved them. Year after year and house after house, we carried those pickles around until they had lived in more homes than a waif out of a Dickens novel.

We did receive a lot of comments. Everytime we moved, whoever it was helping us, would mention how delightful the pickles looked, and we assumed the role of proud owners.

Upstairs and downstairs we moved those pickles. In town and across the country, we moved those pickles. I became quite accustomed to lifting them.

One day, after years of such exercise, we took the bold plunge. We took out one of those jars of pickles and opened it. Suffice it to say they looked better than they tasted. Flat and briny, the taste faintly reminded one of seaweed.

That's when we threw the case in the trash.

Now, ask yourself, "What am I carrying around that I could do better without? What kind of useless garbage am I expending precious energy moving around?"

I have socks in my drawer that I haven't worn since my feet grew two sizes, but I still rummage through them everyday in search for mates of more recent acquisitions.

I have ties so old that they have gone out of style twice.

In the attic, putting stress on the ceiling, we have magazines so old that there aren't any shocking words in them.

We have enough steak knives to have equipped Hannibal's army should it have ever decided to eat one of those elephants.

Now, if any of that hits close enough to home, let's talk about some other kinds of garbage we too often store.

Our spouse says one sentence we don't like, and we pout for three days.

Our child makes a mistake, and although it's been ten years, we still wake up in the middle of the night and wonder when he's going to do it again.

Our dog bit the neighbor. The neighbor says it's all right, but we don't believe him.

We have a problem with a co-worker. So, for the next two weeks we spend our time darting into bathrooms and hiding in doorways to keep from having the inevitable confrontation.

Our Savior died on the cross to cleanse us of the guilt of sin, and all we have to do is repent.

Garbage is heavier than the other material we have to carry. When we tote around garbage, we also have to pack the foolishness that goes with it.

Blessed Are the Disorganized for They Shall Know the Joy of Discovery

I like new laborsaving devices. Not only do we have high-tech gadgets that reduce something like the building of Rome into a routine chore, we also have overhauled the language so that we can reduce major conversations into fifteen-second chats by simply selecting the appropriate words and symbols.

I was in a group when one member described someone who was about to join us as Type A. Everyone then nodded cognizance, as if with that one simple symbol, we knew the history, future, personality, and body type of this person we hadn't even met yet.

How efficient and tidy! Aren't you glad you live in the modern world? With two short words, and one not even a full word, we cut through the process of getting to know someone. Why bother gathering other information to determine whether you want this person as a friend or business associate?

This type of expedient language has great potential. I would like to see us develop symbols to represent another great distinction between two kinds of people—those who know where "it" is, and those who don't.

In the interest of clarity and brevity, we will call the first group "plumbs." You know the type, but for the sake of a definition let's consider some examples.

Plumbs: Plumbs sign their retirement papers with the same fountain pen their parents gave them as a high school graduation gift.

Although the secretary has not had a call for this form for seven years, plumbs can open a file cabinet, reach in, and pull it out.

The plumb in the family who cooks not only knows what's for dinner next Thursday but has already bought the food.

The professional plumb took an aptitude test at three, entered a preprofessional track during kindergarten, joined the firm of choice, and knows what day of the week retirement falls on.

The plumb driver does not dread car-trading time because the title of the old car isn't lost.

When a plumb shops he or she can write a check and accurately record all the relevant information on the stub, including the remaining balance.

On the other hand, we have the rest of the people. In the interest of clarity and brevity, we will call them the "rounds." Let's consider some examples.

Rounds: A round works crossword puzzles with crayons.

When preparing a meal for in-laws, a round has to go to the store six times in the process.

Rounds can't remember whether their desk at work is wood or metal.

Rounds changed majors six times in college and worked in Aspen following graduation.

Rounds remember it's Mother's Day during the morning sermon.

Rounds never carry a map and refuse to ask for directions.

Now that we have established two types of people and labeled them appropriately, we need to consider one more factor that distinguishes them. The plumbs seem to be more financially independent than the rounds. One of the reasons for this is that the plumbs make a lot of money writing books and giving seminars instructing the rounds on how to become plumbs.

I want, however, to speak out for the rounds. I belong to that group. Although it may take us a little longer to get there, and we may get diverted along the way, there is one great advantage to being in this category.

We rounds live our lives in anticipation and celebration of moments of great joy that plumbs don't have. For us rounds, life is made sweet and dear by those special moments when we find "it." I call them the moments of the Joy of Discovery.

For example, when I get ready to go somewhere, it takes me a little longer. I can dress as fast as anybody, but I need a little extra time to search for my watch, wallet, and glasses.

Since I live among a family of plumbs who don't have as much opportunity to celebrate the moments of the Joy of Discovery, I pass them around. In other words, I recruit the family to participate in the search. That way, when we do discover the items, each in a different place in a different part of the house, I share with them my joyous moments, and they acknowledge their appreciation by saying, "Hooray, we can leave now."

I remember why it is that I remain a round. I can't remember what I did with my notes from the seminar.

30

In the Vending Machine of Life, I'm a Bent Coin

Although my research has not yet been declared official, I'm convinced that spring, and especially May, have provoked more poetry through the years than even love and the assassination of Lincoln combined.

I remember, however, a May day that would not inspire much poetry. It was unseasonably hot and dusty, with winds whipping through the new leaves and rearranging the trash that had appeared as street decorations after the last snow melted.

I was driving around so intent on my errands that I forgot to worry about personal needs, and suddenly I realized I was thirsty. By the time of this discovery, my thirst had gone beyond the nuisance stage and had developed into an all-consuming thirst that activates each nerve ending in the mouth and sends messages of despair to the brain.

I couldn't plan ahead. I couldn't concentrate. I couldn't even swallow. I was obsessed with the thought of finding something liquid.

My mind wandered and flitted between images of

84

arid wastelands and an oasis just for me. For a brief moment, I might remember my boyhood when I would spend Saturday afternoons at the movies riding with Tom Mix across the desert trailing a herd of cows. The next brief moment I would imagine myself in the tropics somewhere standing under a waterfall.

Since I was in an isolated area, if such a thing is possible in the suburbs, I knew that getting cool water from a drinking fountain was unlikely, so I decided to search for a soda machine. Eventually, I spotted one standing outside an old garage that was closed for the afternoon.

Finding two quarters in my pocket, I got this sensation that relief was near and my suffering was about to end.

That's when I looked at the machine. "Sixty-five cents," the sign announced. That's when I discovered a truism about sums of money. There are days when sixty-five cents would be too much for a soda, but there are days when a soda is worth ten times that much.

I understood then the economic principle of supply and demand.

The urgent problem was how to get a dime and a nickel. My first thought was to go out to the road and rob a passing motorist. That's when I learned another principle. Ethical restraints diminish as thirst intensifies.

I still had just enough presence of mind left to look in the reserve fund first: I searched the car seats. I found the dime easily enough because it was stuck behind the driver's seat. The nickel was another matter. I had to do major destruction and finally discovered one when I removed the back seat. It was rusty and bent, but it was still a nickel—honest American money.

I inserted the first quarter in the slot. It rolled down the chute and clicked into place. I began to smile. I inserted the second quarter. It rolled and clicked. I began to laugh. I inserted the dime. It too rolled and clicked. I inserted the nickel. It didn't roll, and it didn't click. It stuck. In desperation, I pushed buttons. I kicked. I punched. I beat with my fists. I pleaded. I tried logic, and I tried tears. Nothing worked. The bent coin was stuck, and I went away thirsty.

I wonder how many times I tend to function like that bent coin. Being a little bent isn't necessarily a bad thing in itself. In fact, on some days it might even be a virtue. But being so bent that you can't slide down the slot and click into place makes you worthless, and that leaves a lot of people thirsty.

31

If Your Shoes Don't Fit, Don't Change Feet

I once watched a very fine, experienced teacher try a new teaching procedure—one that allowed students to work together on a project and to assume some ownership for the outcome of their own learning.

Twenty-two eighth graders rolled up their sleeves, tackled the challenge with enthusiasm, and grew intellectually and emotionally in the process. However, three of the class members complained, goofed off, didn't learn, and became a nuisance.

Soon the teacher saw the folly of her ways, dropped the new procedure, and went back to the old teaching methods—where the majority learned a little less and the three troublemakers continued their insubordination.

I once listened to a very fine minister who laced his sermons with jokes and stories that helped people not only get the point but also grow in their relationship with God.

One old veteran church member who hadn't smiled since the day of the stock market crash complained to the rest of the congregation that the minister's sermons lacked depth and intellectual stimulation. As the curmudgeon pointed out to his fellow parishioners, any speech that isn't boring lacks depth.

Of course, the minister's friends overheard the criticism; and in dutiful fulfillment of the first requirements of friendship, they carried the news to him.

So, the minister quit telling jokes and stories and started preaching point by point and on and on. The congregation found time each Sunday morning for snoozing and napping—except for the man who complained, and he soon moved to another church anyway.

As these stories indicate, our response to any situation takes one of three directions: action, reaction, or overreaction.

The third response is a by-product of the age—the age that I have dubbed the Age of Icarus. As you remember from your days in Greek literature class, Icarus was the chap who flew too close to the sun, melting the wax keeping his wings together.

I find that illustration significant in this age of quick fixes and throw away commodities. We want our solutions to work, and to work right now, regardless of the difficulty of the problem. When the solution doesn't work, we throw away the problem.

If the bicycle has a flat tire, we get a new bicycle.

If our children act like the neighbor's children; or even worse, if our children act like we did when we were children, we find ways to keep them occupied rather than to be active with them.

If somebody commercializes a sacred holiday, we get rid of the holiday.

If students don't learn the material the way it is taught, we get rid of the material.

If the shoes don't match the dress, we get a new dress.

If one unreasonable person criticizes us for the way we function, we quit functioning.

If our shoes don't fit, we get new feet. Now you do have to admit that that isn't the most practical way to proceed.

You Don't Know How the Chair Works Until You Sit

When Mary first brought it home, I shook my head and sadly announced, "Surely, you have lost your senses."

It was not an ordinary chair. It was one of those postmodern jobs: low slung with legs sticking out everywhere like a preteen with feet too big. It looked like something the aliens had kicked off the UFO just before they took off again.

I immediately didn't like it, and was afraid of the thing. Its shape and the way it sort of gobbled up any occupants made me afraid it might eat me. Those things do sense our fears, I think.

Now, I'm usually appreciative of Mary's tastes in furniture, and when I'm not appreciative, I'm at least tolerant. Except of course when she buys turkey hot dogs and sheer garbage bags. But I wasn't tolerant with this postmodern, people-eating contraption that she brought home and placed in our living room.

I never sat in it. But Mary did. She would ease down into it, pick her feet up, sigh a warm sigh, and exclaim, "Oh, this is so comfortable." She didn't really mean it. She only said that because she had bought it, and she needed to put on a show.

Throughout the whole ordeal, I was so turned off by the machine that I committed the biggest sin of husbandhood and parentdom. I used the "N" word. I said "Never." "You'll never catch me sitting in that thing," I said with zeal and determination. Now, I have been husband and father long enough to know that you never say never. But that's how distraught I was.

Through the months, the chair and I developed a mutual distrust of each other. If no one was looking, I would kick at it when I would go by, and it bit me once.

One day the inevitable came. I had just returned home, tired from a busy day, with an uncontrollable obsession to work the crossword puzzle in the newspaper. As if by design, there was something in each available seat. My only alternatives were to sit in the space monster, or to stand. I chose to sit.

I eased down into it, wondering if I would ever be seen alive again. Immediately, the chair reached up, grabbed my body, elevated my legs, massaged my back, and brought rest to my weary bones. This was the most comfortable chair I had ever met. Most chairs are chairs, but this one was warm and cordial. Now it has not only become my chair, but it is also my friend. When I am forced to sit in another chair, I find myself apologizing to it.

Now, the question is obvious. Why did it take me months to discover this?

The answer is hard and cold. It's called prejudice.

Prejudice is one of the great banes of our existence. It affects most of the choices we make in life—friends, business associates, heroes, food, cars.

The persuasive argument against prejudice always focuses on the harm it causes the recipient. I want to make another point stemming from the chair affair.

Prejudice is a great incovenience to the practicer as

well. How much of the joy of life had I missed just because I didn't trust the chair enough to sit down?

33

If My Legs Aren't Getting Longer, Why Is the Ground Farther Away?

I first noticed something strange about my legs while bending down to pick up coins. I used to go through life picking up every coin I found—penny, nickel, dime, quarter, Susan B. Anthony dollar. I would always rejoice over my unexpected wealth as you do when you find time left on the parking meter, or when you find an almost-complete edition of today's paper on a bus seat.

One day, however, I realized that the ground was getting farther from the end of my arm, so I began to discriminate. I stopped picking up pennies altogether and found myself wrestling with decisions about nickels. "Surely," I surmised, "my legs must be growing longer."

Having longer legs is not all bad. I've mastered some new disciplines since the growth began. A loose shoelace is just not the nuisance it once was. I find that I can walk patiently for two or three blocks with a loose lace, particularly if I know the shoes are coming off at my destination.

Caterpillars are not the inviting playthings they once were.

My grandchildren don't need as many piggyback rides as my children did—or at least that variety where you get down on all fours and prance around like you're Trigger.

But the greatest achievement of all is that I have whipped the vice of envy. Well, at least I don't envy tall people anymore.

Although my legs are considerably longer than they used to be, I still have just as much trouble changing the light bulb in the bathroom. That added length is no asset at all.

But that's because they're making step stools shorter than they used to.

34

Blessed Are Those Who Wear Comfortable Shoes

I have trouble making plans. I always lose sight of the ultimate outcome and overcommit myself.

I agree for committee duty and lose sight completely of all the time-consuming activity required.

I order the main course and lose sight completely of all the tasty desserts I'd like to try.

I dress every morning for success and lose sight completely of what the weather conditions and my own emotional state might be by 3:00 P.M.

That type of oversight happens every day. You would think that after thirty-four years in the working world, I would learn. I get up, shower, think of my important business with Mr. Important at 3:00 P.M., and don piece by piece my important suit and important shoes.

Wearing my important suit all day long is not a great bother. Wearing my important shoes, however, is a different matter. Important shoes are uncomfortable. Even if you get them big enough to fit, which most important people don't, they still must come in those weird, contorted shapes that in no way even remotely resemble a normal foot.

Thus, after marching around all day in my important and uncomfortable shoes, I cease to feel important, and I begin to feel pretentious. I begin to act pretentious. I begin to take myself too seriously. I might then get defensive, lose patience, and resent others, especially those who seem to be more comfortable than I am.

Consequently, by the time I get to the business meeting, I'm in a bad mood. By that time, compromise is a concept not even in my vocabulary anymore. Neither is understanding or mercy. I have lost all traces of human nobility and all because of those shoes.

Surely, I'm not the only person to fall victim to this trap. I wonder how many other people walk into negotiations with pinched personalities, simply because they put on the wrong shoes that morning. How many librarians threatening court action because a book is overdue, how many traffic cops writing speeding tickets to buggy drivers, how many international arbitrators discussing world peace by threatening war.

It all causes me to stop and ponder. How many hard-hearted thoughts could be avoided, how many wars could be averted, how many committee meetings could be significantly shortened, how many decisions could be reached, and how many lives could be enriched if we could all just plan our day with one simple motto, "Blessed are those who wear comfortable shoes."

Copy Machines Are an Alien Plot

SERGORP: Eureka! Eureka! Eureka!

OZOB: What's all the shouting about in there?

SERGORP: Come look. I've just invented it. My dream of galaxy reign is about to be complete. This is the machine that will eventually destroy the Things on planet Earth.

OZOB: Oh my, it does look deadly and destructive. What do you call it?

SERGORP: It's called a copy machine.

OZOB: Copy machine? That's a strange name for a weapon of destruction. How does it work?

SERGORP: Let me demonstrate. You put a sheet of paper containing important information on this glass; you close the door; you put in some money; you punch the button; the machine roars to life; the light comes on. Presto! You have a perfect copy in this little basket.

OZOB: Yes! I see! I see! But I don't understand. It would seem that this would be good. The Earth Things could make copy after copy. This is constructive and not destructive.

SERGORP: That's the brilliance of my plan. The destruction is so subtle that no one shall ever suspect. Let me show you. First consider the money. The machine will work on two kinds of money—coins or little plastic cards.

OZOB: But how is that destructive? I would think that would be a great convenience.

SERGORP: Only in theory. I will place these machines so that when one has a coin, the machine needs a card; and when one has a card, the machine needs a coin.

OZOB: I'm beginning to see. You seek death by confusion.

SERGORP: Yes! Yes! Never underestimate the deadly force of frustration. But there's more!

OZOB: More! More! I love it. Tell me.

SERGORP: It isn't dependable.

OZOB: What do you mean? It doesn't work?

SERGORP: Oh no, it works most of the time, but it

only fails at crucial moments. Let's suppose an Earth Thing has an important event. He's a businessman late for a meeting, and he needs five copies of a report. He rushes to the machine, puts in his money, and at that crucial moment when copying is most important, the machine doesn't work.

OZOB: It is a very smart machine to fail at the crucial times only, but what goes wrong?

SERGORP: Much. It runs out of paper. It runs out of fluid. The light burns out. The cylinder cracks. The A-frame is bent.

OZOB: Oh, I see the plan now. You are indeed brilliant to have invented such a machine. It will become a part of the culture. The culture will accept it as a necessity, and it will be so inconsistent that frustration will set in. Frustration will ruin the Earth. What a plot! You deserve the title of the Ultimate Fiend of the Galaxy.

SERGORP: Oh! You're too kind. But there's more.

OZOB: More! How villainous can you be?

SERGORP: Oh, yes! The confusion and frustration is only on the surface. The real destruction is even more subtle.

OZOB: Quickly, tell me so I too can enjoy the plot.

SERGORP: This machine will steal the one thing that makes Earth Things special and the only thing that can really save them.

OZOB: What is that?

SERGORP: This machine will steal the personal touch out of relationships. This great copy machine will do that so well that Earth Things won't even know it's happening.

OZOB: I don't think I understand.

SERGORP: The theft of person-to-person encounters will happen in every walk of life. When a government official wants to brief his or her staff, they aren't called together for discussion. They each receive a copied note. The note may have the facts, but it can't smile. It can't answer questions. The staff respond to the note, but they are responding to orders and not to a personality. When clients come for service, government officials will be programmed to say things like, "I'm sorry. That's not my department." "The deadline was yesterday." "You didn't fill it out correctly." "The latest communique plainly says. . . ."

Businesspersons will no longer meet face-to-face to seal contracts. They will copy and send things through another hideous invention called the fax. The copy machine and the fax machine working together will replace the handshake. Old-timers will sit around and recall, "I remember the old days when we could just make a deal and shake hands over it. That was good enough—just a handshake. We didn't need all this darned paperwork and all these mechanical monsters around."

The younger ones will only chuckle at the thought of archaic customs. They will make a note, copy it, and fax it just to prove their point.

Within one generation the custom of the handshake will be completely forgotten. Earth Things will have no reason to touch each other anymore. They will grow isolated, and they won't even know why. They will begin to distrust each other. They will get defensive and lonely.

Teachers will put their lessons on paper, copy them, and teach, not through eyes and smiles and voices with personality, but through something called the "handout." Students will sit at their desks with ears closed and do the handouts. In the process, they will learn an important lesson. Wisdom and thought and great ideas can be reduced to paper. The printed word will become the source of learning and authority.

The Earth Things will cut down their trees to make more paper so they can make more copies. They will destroy their personal relations and their ecologies at the same time.

OZOB: Stop it! Stop it! This is the most wicked plot I have ever heard! You are indeed brilliant.

SERGORP: But there's more.

OZOB: More? How can there be more?

SERGORP: This is the best part of all.

OZOB: I'm not sure I want to hear, but tell me.

SERGORP: With the copy machine, the Earth Things will pride themselves on their progress. They will make copies and copies. They won't need to make decisions about what's important and what isn't. They just make multiple copies of everything, regardless of its worth. Once something is copied, it will look important even if it isn't. The Earth Things will say, "This is the Information Age," and they will work late into the night. No longer will they sit around and tell stories. They won't sit on creek banks and throw pebbles in the water. They won't sleep enough. Every moment of every day they will leaf through the copies, trying to assimilate the information, and one day the big moment will come.

OZOB: The big moment?

SERGORP: The final scene—the moment of destruction.

OZOB: What will happen?

SERGORP: *Their brains will explode!*

Blessed Are the Ignorant for They Shall Never Be Bored

My most prized possession is my large supply of ignorance. I'm a real collector. Every day I add to the stock.

It's really quite easy and doesn't require much investment. I amble through a library and glance at all those books I'll never get around to reading. I think of the wisdom contained there and the efforts poured out to get that wisdom on paper. And the depth of my ignorance grows.

I drive down the street of a town where I have never been before, and I look into the faces of all those people that I will never meet and never get to know. I wonder why they cry and why they laugh. And the depth of my ignorance grows.

I stand in my back yard and watch the sunset. I wonder how that same sunset looks to those watching from atop the Himalayas or from a sailing ship somewhere in the Pacific or from Death Valley. And the depth of my ignorance grows.

I like discovering my ignorance. I wouldn't have it any other way. Whenever I meet the knowledgeable, they seem so bored with it all that I feel sorry for them.

The other day I sat in the back of a high school classroom for fifty-five minutes while the teacher spoke of something that didn't seem to be too important to him. In that fifty-five minutes, the teacher said "Okay?" fifty-seven times. During that fifty-five minutes two girls passed four different notes. One guy counted the ceiling tiles. A girl took her left shoe off and scratched her toes. The crack in the chalkboard appeared to grow wider as the sun shone from a different angle. And a mouse sneaked out of the closet, looked around, listened to part of the lecture, and went home again.

All that in less than an hour. But as I walked out the door, I overheard two of the students in deep conversation.

"That was bor-r-ring," they said and nodded in agreement with each other.

The other day, my good friend, a knowledgeable type, told me that the party he had attended the night before had been boring. I was so shocked at the concept that I couldn't even remember the word, "oxymoron." How can such a thing be, at a place where there are people to meet, finger food to eat, coffee cups to balance on a knee, and ideas to think.

Maybe one of the reasons why I'm not bored is that I'm afraid to use the term. I'm afraid that if I say I'm bored, God will think I'm blasphemous. He'll think that what I'm really saying is, "God, I don't like the way you put the universe together. Why didn't you throw in some exciting things to keep me entertained?"

Well, I don't feel that way, and I don't even want to get started. Every experience is new, and if it doesn't seem new at least it has new ramifications and perspectives to discover. Every person on earth is unique, and there is more to learn about people than I will ever be able to know. If I get finished looking at the big things, I can look at the little ones. All the while, I'll just keep adding to my stockpile of ignorance and feeling sorry for the knowledgeable.

37

Include the Mouth in Disarmament Talks

In the region where I spent my boyhood, it didn't snow much; but when the snow did come, I loved to make snowballs. I just enjoy three dimensional geometrical objects, and making snowballs was a fun challenge because the snow was usually moist and packable.

I launched into making each individual ball with the goal that maybe this would be the snowball of all snowballs.

One day after a light snow had fallen, I picked up the challenge and had amassed a sizable stockpile when my older sister came outside, saw my activity, snarled her upper lip, and said, "You won't hit me with a snowball. I'll tell Momma."

I bombed her. I really had never thought of even the possibility of throwing those snowballs at anyone until she mentioned it; but at the suggestion of the idea, I bombed her.

Of course, she went and told Mom, and I got a spanking. Then my sister said in her sing-song way,

"You got a spanking. You got a spanking." So I kicked her.

It was at this point that I realized something about world peace and international ethics. It wasn't my arsenal that started all the hostility, but her mouth.

When we talk of times when nations shall live in harmony and peoples of the world will sing and drink soda together, we always talk of disarmament.

I'm sure that's where we need to start, but no true peace can ever come until we finally silence the vocal cannons that boom wild and separate us.

Somebody named Anonymous once said, "Sticks and stones may break my bones, but words will never hurt me." That person was either an insensitive oaf or he was whistling in the dark.

Words do hurt deeply, and they may hurt for a lifetime.

In the world of missiles, words are surely the most devastating. For one thing, there are no interception devices—no Patriots to knock your words out of the air. A word, once it has been launched, flies true to its target and does its damage without fail.

The effects of word warfare last a long time. Words have the possibility of continuing to do damage for years and even generations after they have first hit their target, and there are no simple ways to rebuild after the devastation.

Now, almost a half-century later, my sister and I

have grown up. I love my sister. We talk together. We play together, and I never have a malicious thought about her. Except when it snows.

38

When It's Cold in Your Heart, Open a Window

Our sighs are the windows to our hearts. There are warm sighs and cold sighs. One can hear and know the difference.

There are the sighs of a mother looking in on her sleeping children, and those are warm.

There are the sighs of a weary worker finding a seat on the bus, and those are warm.

There are the sighs of a diligent student who has just finished a test.

There are the sighs of two friends parting. Although there are tears in their eyes, the sighs are warm because these friends would still rather be parting than never to have met.

There are sighs that come when the job is finished, when the meal is cooked, and when fresh water cools a summer thirst.

These are the warm sighs because they radiate from warm hearts.

There also are cold sighs—the sighs of a person watching a train go by, of the second driver to spot one parking place, of a rejected friend, of a salesman who didn't close the deal, of a son or daughter watching a parent get old, and of a parent watching a child stay young too long.

One of the objectives of a caring person is to turn the cold sighs into warm sighs, and the method to achieve this is found in the first principle of thermo-dynamics. Warmth is unselfish. It likes to share it-self, so when warmth touches something colder, the coldness becomes warmer.

That's the first principle of happiness. When it's warmer outside your heart than inside, open a window. Then you can sigh a sigh of warmth.

Smugness Is the Luxury of Middle Age

My mother has an old dog who long ago passed middle age. His hair has turned gray, his eyes have glazed over, and his teeth have fallen out.

Besides that he doesn't hear too well. I think that might be the reason he has this compulsion to be close to my mother all the time. He seems to want to be in the same room with her every moment.

My mother feeds her dog in the kitchen. She puts his biscuits in his bowl out by the cupboard, and then she goes back into the television room to watch, sew, and nap. Until just recently, the dog had to go into the kitchen to eat, and was separated from her for that period of time.

The other day he invented a strategy to avoid being alone. When Mom pours his food in his bowl, he runs in, gets a big mouthful, comes back to the television room, spits the food out, and sits there to eat in the company of my mother.

Obviously, that old dog learned a new trick, which either breaks a law of nature or a law of old adages. Whichever, I think that dog should be made a national hero and given a medal by the president. Can you see the headlines? "Old Dog Learns New Trick!"

That sounds fine for the dog kingdom, but I'm not sure it's ever going to catch on in the human world.

Everyday I hear the protests.

"Don't put that computer in my office. I'll never learn to run one of those things!"

"What do you mean, remodel the church? I've sat in this very same pew every Sunday morning for the last thirty years."

"I know that may be all the rage, but can I just have my plain old striped tie back?"

"Oh, just cut it like you always do, I guess."

"So why do you want to go all the way to South America to teach school when there are perfectly good schools right here?"

"No, thanks. No quiche for me. I'm a meat and potatoes person myself."

The people with letters after their names and hard to spell words on their office doors have come up with some scientific reasons for this kind of talk. They tell us that we dread transitions, don't take enough risks, and are afraid of change.

Since I don't really know any fancy psychological terms for what happens, I am going to apply a simple word to describe our plight. We get smug.

It seems to me that that's the trap of middle age. We get so comfortable with who we are that we're afraid even to think about who we might become. We move into the community of the comfortable and like the neighborhood so much that we just decide never to move again.

After a while, we do fear feeling old too soon, so we do something really bizarre. We get a car with a stick shift and buy a silk shirt. Then people accuse us of having a mid-life crisis.

The fear of the accusation of a mid-life crisis is the unkindest cut of all because it too often frightens us into stagnation. As I remember from my high school biology class about a half-century ago, growth is one of the characteristics of all living things.

When we quit growing, we're dead. That's the luring danger of middle age.

40

The Difference Between a Hole and a Rut Is Open Ended

The one thing worse than falling into a hole is falling into a rut. When you fall into a hole, you suddenly land with a splash and a jolt, and you say, "I've just hit bottom."

When you fall into a rut, you ease in gradually and don't even know you're on the bottom until you're so comfortable you don't much feel like climbing out.

You may get some idea that you're in a rut, but because there aren't any ends to be seen or any obstacles ahead, you just keep plugging forward telling yourself that maybe you really are on top of the world.

There are, however, some tell-tale signs to indicate you're in a rut.

- Your best friends are all snakes.
- Other people are always dumping things on top of you.
- You dream about being at work, and you wake up to find that you weren't dreaming after all.
- The highlight of your day is reading the TV schedule in the morning newspaper.
- You think about doing some exercises, but you can't find the Jane Fonda video.
- You have memorized the words on the back of the cereal box.
- You can tell which sock fits which foot.
- There is a pew at church, which through years of use, has taken on the exact contour of your body.
- You don't own stone-washed jeans.
- You still have 78 rpm records, and you know how to waltz.
- You use the same logic with your grandchildren that didn't work with your children.
- You sit in the rocking chair, but you're too tired to make it rock.
- People tell you that you're in a rut, and you don't believe them.

Coming to your senses and recognizing that you're in a rut is a major accomplishment. Too often, moving forward in a rut masquerades as progress, so detection is always a challenge. Accepting the idea that you're in a rut is only the beginning of the end of the problem.

Getting out of a rut is another matter. If you turn around and go the other way, you only make progress backwards. The only way to get out of a rut is to turn perpendicular to it and climb. Only then might you realize that you've been in over your head.

You Could Be the Parent of a Monkey Who Doesn't Like Show Business

Have you ever known a monkey in any job other than show business? Have you ever wondered if monkey parents have the same problems as human parents?

"What did you do in school today, Dear?"

"Nothin."

"Well, what did the teacher teach you?"

"I dunno."

"What do you mean, 'You don't know?' Surely she taught something."

"Yeah, stuff."

"And what kind of stuff was it, Dear?"

"You know like, just stuff."

"Was it interesting?"

"I dunno."

"What do you mean, 'You dunno'?"

"I forgot."

"Well, did you learn something important like peanut catching? That was always one of my favorite subjects when I was your age. And the teacher said I was good at it too. Did she teach you that?"

"Nah."

"Maybe you learned the cute scamper. I remember once we studied the cute scamper for two weeks, and we all got it perfect. Did she teach you that?"

"Nah."

"Oh, I remember a great lesson—limb dangling. That was my worst subject. But it might have not been my fault. I once heard a psychologist say that many young monkeys have a limb-dangling learning block. I think I must have had that. Did she teach you limb dangling?"

"Nah."

"Well, just exactly what did that teacher teach today?"

"Thermodynamics and propulsion."

"What?"

"You know, like stuff."

"Why are you studying that kind of material?"

"I dunno."

"Well, how is that ever going to help you in show business? What are these schools coming to these days? Why don't they teach you kids what you need to know?"

"I need to know this."

"What on earth for?"

"I'm gonna be a rocket scientist."

"Yeah, sure! And I'm a brain surgeon."

"No, I made up my mind. Like wow! That's what I'm gonna be!"

"You had better stop that kind of talk right now! When the time comes, you'll go into show business just like everybody else."

"But I don't wanna."

"What do you mean? You don't want to join your father's profession and your grandfather's and your great grandfather's before him!"

"I don't wanna."

"Well, let me tell you. If you think for one moment that you're better than your father, well, young man, you've got another think coming. Rocket scientist! Where did you get such an idea anyway? It must be from your father's side of the house. Now, what do you have for homework?"

"Nothin."

If monkeys are anything like humans, the little one

probably grew up and entered show business anyway, and married someone just like his mom, and produced offspring who dreamed of being a rocket scientist and answered every question with "I dunno."

To Catch a Rat, Stand in One Place and Look Like Cheese

In an old country store deep in the heart of hill country, a man of some years sat on a pop bottle case and with passion in his voice told me of the gentlemanly sport of fox hunting.

"Along about the deepest darkest hour of a cold winter night, when the sky is full of stars and the moon makes shadows in the woods, we meet in our spot out where nobody could find it unless they knowed about it, and we turn our dogs loose. The whole pack—Arlo's three, Bertram's two, and Winiford's three, and my two.

"Then, out there in the woods where the trees make the only noise, we build us a fire out of pine knots, and we just sit around the good-smelling fire while the dogs commence to hunt. And soon they'll spy an old fox way back in the dark somewhere, and we say, 'Let the fox hunt begin.'

"The fox runs, and those old dogs get on the trail, and while we sit around that fire just listening, those old dogs begin to telegraph us back reports. They bay and sing something fierce, and we all know by the sound of their voices where they're running, who's hot and who's not. There ain't nothing in the world like sitting around a fire in the deep woods listening to the dogs hunt a fox."

Like naive outsiders too often do, I interrupted his story with a stupid question, "What do you do when you catch the fox?"

His whole countenance changed. It wasn't a look of anger or even a look of shock. It was a look of disappointment. How could I be so misunderstanding and gruesome?

"We never catch the fox," he said quietly, and that was the end of our conversation.

After thinking about it for a few years, I have decided that this country sport of fox hunting is just the opposite of the urbanized sport of the rat race.

As best as I can tell, the objective of the rat race is hurry. You eat your meals standing, carry a briefcase so that you can have portable work, drive recklessly to make appointments, run through airports, and you never allow yourself to get more than twenty feet from a telephone.

But nobody ever catches the rat!

Aren't sports fun, once you understand the finer points of the game!

43

Impatience Is the Luxury of Youth

Planning for the future is a relative activity. When you're fifty-five, it's saving for retirement ten years hence. When you're twenty-one and a college senior, it's knowing where you're going to be working three months after graduation. When you're fourteen, it's having a firm idea of which mall you're going to hang out at Friday night.

We often speak of a "generation gap," and we search for something specific to describe it—the loudness of music, the length of hair, or which gender looks best with earrings.

Maybe all the while the major difference between the young and the old is this perspective of time.

It seems almost ironic. When you're young and don't have much time behind you but a lot ahead of you, you're impatient to make things happen right now. When you get old and you have a lot of time behind you and only a little left ahead, you don't mind waiting a bit.

Anyone who has any business with the younger set knows about this gap.

Even the most inexperienced teacher has had a student impatiently hold up his hand and demand permission to go to the bathroom. When the teacher asks the classic question, "How bad do you have to go?" the answer is always even more impatient: "Bad, and right now!"

Breathes there anywhere a parent who has not had at least one child say, "Oh, Mom, there's a really important meeting at school. You need to be there in fifteen minutes"?

Anyone who has ever transported children in any conveyance that even slightly resembles a station wagon has learned the agony of the every-five-minute query, "How long till we get there?"

And who among us hasn't had the delight of watching Miss Teenage Princess put goop on her face and look in the mirror ten minutes later to see if the pimple is gone yet?

Yes, they are an impatient species, the young. Those of us who remember what we were doing when Kennedy was assassinated will never fully understand them.

On the other hand, they don't understand us either. They don't understand why it's better to wait until tomorrow to buy something.

They don't understand people who dread their next birthday.

They don't understand doing research that requires more than one night in the library or reading a book that has more than 120 pages.

They don't understand watching a television program that takes thirty minutes to get to the punch line or listening to music that soothes instead of stimulates.

So, there does seem to be a generation gap. There probably always has been and always will be. But maybe that's not all bad. The young can't wait as long as we do, but they don't hate as long either. They can't stay as long as we do, but it doesn't take them as long to get there.

We need somebody to read the long books and somebody to read the short ones. We need somebody to watch the five-part television shows and somebody to watch David Letterman. We need somebody to move the world along faster than it's going, and we need someone to slow it down a bit.

Isn't it refreshing to consider that in God's wisdom age groups were made just like they are?

The next time you hear a wee voice in the backseat plea "How long till we get to Grandma's house?", you can smile, remember a time that doesn't seem so long ago when you asked a similar question, thank

God for the impatience that provoked it, and answer as casually as age permits, "Five minutes sooner than the last time you asked."

44

At Least the Chicken Crossed the Road

I feel sorry for the people who are always the butt of jokes. Maybe that's why I've spent some time worrying about the infamous chicken. I've heard about it all my life.

In all my school years, as a student and as a teacher, there probably was not a month that went by that someone didn't come up to me with a grin, and deliver the masterpiece of the day.

"Do you know why the chicken crossed the road?" He or she would ask, obviously hoping that I didn't.

"No," I would answer. Then I would wait for my daily dosage of childish humor.

"He wanted to lay it on the line."

"Kentucky Fried Chicken was building on this side."

"He was taking ballet and needed to practice jumping cars."

121

"To hold his pants up."

You may think that last one doesn't make much sense, but among rejoinders that school kids find funny, that one made more sense than most.

I understand that humor is humor and shouldn't be taken too seriously. However, I want to point out that there is an overlooked and vital lesson in those little chicken jokes, which is essential to the survival of the human race.

The chicken crossed the road. Isn't that inspiring? This chicken started into the joke on one side of the road and came out of the joke on the other side. This is clearly a determined bird, a fellow of action.

Sick humorists and pseudo-philosophers can sit around for hours and guess about motives if they want to, but I want to cheer his action and daring.

Through the years, I have learned that there are two kinds of chickens—those that cross the road and those who don't cross but stand around and wonder why the others did. Through the years, I have learned that there are two kinds of people—those who do things and others who make fun of the first group's accomplishments.

When I think of that first kind, two great inventors come to mind—a fellow named Edison and one named Oscar Feddleman.

The first man had an idea for making a light that used electricity instead of oil.

The second invented a device that would prevent football players from losing their contacts on the field. He pierced their eyelids and attached a string through the eyelid and lens so that when the contacts fell out, they would just dangle on the player's cheeks.

Let me guess what you're doing about now. You're nodding approval about Edison but you're hissing and booing old Oscar. Well, that's a bad case of bandwagoning. You know that Edison's project is going to work, but you aren't sure about Oscar's, so you're laughing at him.

Let me assure you that Oscar has more of the Edison qualities than the laughers and gossipers do. Both inventions grew out of the same human spirit. One just had a little better design.

If nobody crosses the road, if nobody risks the absurd, this old world isn't going to go very far.

Let's applaud the chicken and be honest with the jokesters. Does anybody really care *why* he crossed the road?

45

Don't Ask—I Don't Understand Why Either

When Alyssa, my three-year-old granddaughter, was one year old, walking with her was a rewarding experience. In those days she was in her One-Word-Solution period. Regardless of the natural phenomenon, she had a one-word pronouncement for the mystery of the universe.

She would stop occasionally, with rapt attention admire a crack in the sidewalk, and christen her discovery, "Cwak."

She would point to the flying object overhead, whatever it might be, and proclaim, "Duck."

She would hear a dog barking in the distance and say, "Woof."

Now that she is three years old, walking with Alyssa has become a totally new experience. She is now into her Critical-Thinking-and-Natural-Philosophy period.

I might point to an object flying overhead and pronounce "duck."

And she says with twinkles in her eyes and sincerity in her tone, "Why?"

I say, "Because it is a duck. It lives on a pond and flies around."

And she says, "Why?"

I say, "Because that's what ducks do. That's their purpose in life. That's the way God made them."

And she says, "Why?"

Walking with Alyssa during this period of her development has been quite educational. I have learned that there is a lot about ducks that I don't know. In fact, there is a lot about the world I don't know.

I know how ducks fly, but I don't know why they would rather be on the other side of the pond in the first place.

I know why there are cracks in the sidewalk, but I don't know why concrete expands when it gets hot.

I don't know why adults throughout centuries have always thought the present generation of kids is softer or ruder or not as well educated as they were.

I don't know why some people are cruel.

I don't know why $2+2=4$.

I don't know why it's blue for boys and pink for girls.

I don't know why life rhymes with wife.

I don't know why a cricket game takes three days.

I don't know why you can say "myself" but can't say "hisself."

I don't know why the people who are the presidents of things are the presidents of things.

And I don't know why three-year-old girls ask "Why?" all the time.

I'm glad they do. I'm also glad that I don't know why because as long as I don't there will always be a bit of a three-year-old in me too.

46

History Will Know Us by the Men Who Wore Neckties

Have you ever noticed how we identify every era of history with some little special characteristic that gives the whole period its distinction?

I'm not sure I know the reason for that. Maybe it comes from our tendency to simplify everything. Maybe we learned about that period of time when we had other things on our minds, and we're lucky to remember simplistic labels.

Regardless of the reason, labeling eras is a harmless little activity that does provide convenience. We all remember how it works.

The Greeks thought a lot and had giant debates.

The Romans fought a lot and moved like a turtle.

During the Dark Ages, the sun didn't shine.

In the medieval times, the church was like the weather is now. Everybody talked about it, but nobody did much about it.

During the Renaissance, people read a lot.

During the Feudal Period, there was an epidemic of dragons.

In the Enlightenment, everybody either discovered something or invented it.

The Puritans went to church all the time.

In the antebellum South, people grew cotton and had parties.

In the last part of the nineteenth century, everybody moved to the city, got a bathtub, and worked in a factory.

During the 1930s, the wind blew dust around all the time.

During the 1940s, everybody was patriotic.

And that brings us to the present age. Five hundred years from now when school children study us for an exam, what will be the little tag of identity they will attach to us for convenience and recall?

We won't be the age that read a lot, or that was benevolent and kind, or discovered new places, or went to church much.

No, there has to be something more representative of the theme of our civilization. Because I am not very good at seeing the future, I hesitate to guess what those people might settle upon, but I have this nagging fear that we will be remembered as the civilization of men who wore neckties.

Is there anything more representative of our lifestyle than that? The necktie is a pervasive factor in describing the character of our civilization. There are those who tell me that we are the Age of Convenience, and they cite packaged food and throw-away products as proof. But men still wear neckties.

There are those who tell me that we are the Age of Practicality and Pragmatism—a people more focused on the ends rather than the means. But the bottom line is, men still wear neckties.

There are those who tell me that this is the Information Age—that we are a knowing people, always searching and experimenting. But men still wear neckties.

Have you ever wondered what these little strips of cloth tied around men's necks—within the boundaries of rigid rules of knot construction, color, and length—say about us?

Since some identify us as a Practical Age, I tried to find utilitarian purposes for the necktie. Consider the list.

1. In an age when most people are overweight anyway, ties detract attention from a big belly.

2. When we are wearing a necktie, people know at first glance who among us has any sense of color coordination and artistic taste.

3. The necktie craze provides work for millions of silkworms who would otherwise be unemployed.

4. A necktie is a constant reminder that we should never become totally comfortable in the presence of others.

There are those who would point at the neckties and accuse men of being a pretentious bunch. And there are times when I almost agree with them—when I'm in a hurry getting dressed and the ends don't come out right, when I'm wearing the blue suit and can only find the brown tie, when I spill chili on my tie just before an important meeting. At these times I do question the practice and scoff a bit at our seeming pretentiousness.

Maybe neckties aren't all bad, though. Maybe wearing a necktie is just one small symbol that reminds us that we are still civilized.

You Don't Know What Lonesome Is Until You Go on a Diet

BUSINESS LUNCH—doesn't that sound exciting? It just smacks of success, progress, and power. Important people have business lunches.

The really important people have business break-fasts on days when success runs so rampant they couldn't get everything in during the previous day's lunch.

For the profoundly and terminally successful, there are even business dinners, where the measure of success turns into a competition of who can buy the most and eat the most.

I started a small business. As the years progressed, the business improved until it got good, and I got fat. After a while, I got tired of being fat, so I went on a diet. I got svelte. And the business fell into the whirling eddies of a recession.

Who ever would have thought that it would come to this? We are now living in a civilization in which business acumen includes a healthy appetite and a metabolism that can burn up more calories than we can safely eat.

This isn't just a criterion for success in the world of commerce. You never realize that food is at the core of our culture until you start eating selectively.

Not only has my business suffered, but I don't even get invited to parties anymore. The host or hostess try explanations like "I know you're on a diet, and I don't want you to be tempted." But that's a malnourished excuse. I know the real reason. Their egos suffer when you don't clean your plate and when you turn down their special recipe of homemade German chocolate cake.

As a parent dieting is a liability. The kids say, "Let's have some family fun. Let's all go down to High Cholesterol Fast Food Emporium and pork out."

When I reject that offer with an empty, "I'm sorry. I don't much feel like going out tonight," they propose an alternative.

"Let's order in seventeen different kinds of pizza and eat two slices each."

When I reject that proposal, they say, "You're no fun anymore." They then go out to search for a substitute dad.

It seems to me that this underlying obsession with food is more than an innocent cultural glitch. This is a domestic problem severe enough to deserve congressional investigation. In this age when fat-clogged arteries are this country's number one health problem, we simply have to begin searching for an alternative.

How would it be if we made exercise the social forum for business? Rather than business lunches, we could have business mile runs, and we could cut deals over a set of one hundred sit-ups.

Can you see the possibilities? Hot showers would take the place of after-dinner mints, and the antacid people could make a fortune selling Maalox Muscle Ointment.

Exercise is definitely an improvement over food. But there is still one minor problem. Like eating, exercising is still something of a self-indulgent activity, and it would be possible to become an exercise glutton.

Perhaps the solution would be to build a society of businesspersons wheeling and dealing while engaged in community service. Let's ponder how this would work.

"You have a nice proposal there, Barnes. Let's find some nice out-of-the-way spot on Route 40 and discuss it while we're walking along the roadside picking up trash."

"Your offer of $800 billion for my company seems fair enough. Let's get together tonight down at the Y and hammer out all the details while monitoring the local school's Homework Hotline."

For family fun, we could spend an evening raking leaves at the park or shoveling snow at the hospital.

Teenagers could get into the act. Rather than gathering inside the mall to hang out while sipping sodas and munching chocolate chip cookies, they could go outside the mall and spend the evening helping forgetful middle-aged men find the car they lost in the parking lot.

I can imagine the results now—a world more beautiful, people with joy in their hearts, and dieters as the life of the party. In my imagination I might be able to withstand the social humiliation that comes from eating selectively.

48

I Remember My Childhood—It's Yesterday I've Forgotten

Once when I was a boy, I sat on a creek bank under a cottonwood tree and fished with a worm on a hook about four inches under the bobber. An old striped bass came up, grabbed it, and hooked himself. I was elated with my catch—until I looked into his eyes and saw him pleading with me. So I took him off the line, threw him back in, and went home whistling.

Yesterday, I flew into some city (I can't remember which because all airport hotels look the same to me) and I did big business. I sat across the table from this guy and dangled my bait until I hooked him. I was elated with my catch. When I get time to review my notes, I'll remember exactly what advantage I gained.

When I was a boy, my mother made her own bread, and she let me eat some fresh out of the oven. Because it was too hot to cut, I tore off a piece, plastered it with freshly churned butter and homemade apple butter, and ate the feast of kings.

Yesterday, I had lunch in some fine restaurant, and

I had fish, or maybe chicken, and I think there was a vegetable. I can't remember.

When I was a boy, I read *Call of the Wild*. I followed the dogs and felt the wind blowing in my face. I made imaginative shelters against the cold and smelled the food cooking.

Yesterday, I read a book on the plane. I don't remember the title. It was pretty good, though, at least for the time I was reading it.

In recent years, I've discovered an interesting phenomenon. The older I get the clearer my childhood becomes. Maybe ten years from now, I'll remember yesterday.

In the meantime, I am having fun recalling the stories of my childhood. I have even thought about writing some of them down, but I can't remember where I left my pen.

When I was a boy, I kept my pens in the holes of an old distributor cap that sat on the dresser next to the bed.

49

I'm a Victim of Child Persuasion

I am luckier than most frustrated people. My encourager makes house calls. Alyssa, my granddaughter, comes to see me.

The last time she came, I was out in the back trying to cut unruly branches off the old apple tree. To say that I'm not good at such things would be an understatement on a par with saying that Custer was not good at scouting for Indians or that Napoleon was not good at keeping the supply lines open. The quantity of my being not good at gardening is measurable and large.

Alyssa came to watch. With the fear of doing more harm than good, I took the saw in hand and started the pruning process. "Oh, Grandpa," the little one said in complete objectivity. "You are so smart." And to prove her right, I worked skillfully and boldly until I had finished hacking off the unnecessary branches.

Then I faced the task of lifting those heavy branches over a wall onto the compost pile. I strained and struggled with one of the lighter ones, and Alyssa said, "Oh, Grandpa, you're so strong."

I soon completed the whole job.

It's amazing to see how much energy and ingenuity one can find when one is trying to live up to a grandchild's expectations.

Such expectations are about the most powerful form of persuasion I have encountered during this period of life, when my waistline is more than half my age. I have begun to wonder about its commercial potential.

As anyone who has read a newspaper headline or owns a television channel remote clicker knows, this country is in serious trouble because of worldwide perceptions about how we work. According to those perceptions, the Japanese build better automobiles; the Koreans make better clothes; and the Swiss make better wristwatches and army knives.

Whether these perceptions are true or not, American industry needs to discover a renewed enthusiasm for work and production. We need an inspiring persuasive technique to recharge our batteries. I recommend grandchildren in the workplace.

Now imagine this picture: The assembly line is spitting the whatzits by at record pace. The workers, experienced people in their late forties and early fifties, bend over and work quickly and deftly putting the refining touches on each minute part. They grow weary from the stress and the pace and the tedium.

Just as they begin to tire and productivity slows down, small children on break from their own studies or play could rush in for a moment and shout, "Oh, Grandpa, you're so smart." "Oh, Grandma, you're so strong."

If that kind of persuasion is as effective with those workers as it was with me during my tree-pruning experience, Japanese industry will be bankrupt in a matter of months.

50

Nature's Idea of Quality Contains a Pecking Order Clause

Somewhere the old man had found an old bench that had once been a school bus seat, and he put it in the shade of his sweet gum tree. There we sat that afternoon and profitably spent our time whittling and talking and watching his chickens peck in the year.

We didn't stir much, the two of us, but the chickens brought movement to the scene. In a hurry going nowhere, they scampered about chasing bugs and grasshoppers and gobbling small pebbles in a sort of frenzy of competition for those things around them in abundance.

They were a varied group, those chickens in the yard. There were red ones and white ones and dappled ones. There were the big ones and the nondescript ones and the little ones and exotic ones—those with feathers on their legs and those without.

The old man knew each one personally. He called them all by given names, and with the kind of enthusiasm that parents show when they speak of their children, he talked of eating habits, nesting schedules, and coop community.

To demonstrate a point, he rose slowly, ambled over to a bag, pulled out some grain, and poured it into a small trough. This action brought a reaction similar to that which occurs when a department store manager announces that a special table has just been marked down from half price. The chickens gathered so quickly that it seemed there were more at the trough than had been in the whole yard.

They cackled and clucked and pecked at each other in the chaos of individuality and anarchy. One lone hen, however, walked up slowly and stood outside the circle. She was not bigger than most nor more beautiful. As best as I could tell, she was just a chicken. But when the others spotted her standing there, they stepped aside and let her walk through the crowd to the trough, where she selected the choicest pieces of grain.

"That's Henrietta," he told me. "She's my best

layer—two-hundred-forty eggs a year, a good fifteen more than any other bird on the place. And she gets to eat first. It's called pecking order."

He paused and stretched, clutching his hands together in front of him, and added a commentary. "It's a shame that humans aren't as smart as chickens."

I suppose there is some kind of economic theory in the old man's comment, but since I don't understand economics any better than I understand where the wind comes from, I'd like to apply the implied principle to parenthood.

A young man held up a baby boy and proudly announced to me, "This is my first son. I am going to have four more so I can have my own basketball team."

As his wife stood by with that look of "We'll discuss this later," the new father added, "And I'm going to be a good father. I'm going to treat them all exactly alike."

As I thought about what he said, I remembered a time long ago when I, too, planned to become the perfect parent and treat all my children alike. No one could have told me that such a thing was not only impossible but actually unfair.

Not even any two chickens are exactly alike. Just ask Henrietta.

51

If Humans Were as Smart as Cows, There Would Be No Need for Political Science

Some jobs can be accomplished alone, but some jobs require help and cooperation. Scratching your back is of the latter category.

Regardless of how slim you are, regardless of how long your arms are, regardless of how lithe you are, there are some parts of your back that are inaccessible to your own hands. For itches in those remote spots, you need help. And good help is so hard to find these days.

Navigating through traffic in cities and on back roads is also easier with someone to help. Mary is a master in the art of orienteering. When we drive somewhere, she always sits in the copilot's seat and handles direction.

With me steering and her at control central, we have navigated the L.A. freeway system, the streets of Boston on a Saturday night, and the back roads of West Virginia. In all that time and in all those places, we have never been lost. We might have been confused a time or two, but we have never been lost.

140

I shall never forget the day we spent in Tapei, Taiwan. Mary matter-of-factly announced that she would look up an old friend. I scoffed as husbands are sometimes inclined to do when faced with preposterous announcements.

"Dear, you are in a strange city with three million people. You will never find your friend in all this."

But Mary found her friend, and it took all of ten minutes. This woman is amazing—except when it comes to the geography of my back. In that region she has absolutely no sense of direction.

"Mary," I shout with the urgency of exquisite pain, "scratch my back on the right shoulder blade." She scratches the left.

"Mary," I plead, "scratch my back on the lower vertebrae." She massages my shoulders. Even the best help, those who take on the job out of a sense of love as well as duty, don't always bring satisfaction.

On the other hand, cows, which are of a higher intellectual order than humans, have solved the dilemma of the itching back with sheer ingenuity. When their backs itch, they find a tree branch, a half-open barn door, a piece of fence, or some other protruding object to crawl under, and they scratch for themselves. That's why you never see one cow scratching another cow's back.

I think I might get some buttons and beads and a piece of strong twine and make a low-hanging, suspended contraption to crawl under when my back itches. Think of all the agony I will spare myself plus all the time and frustration it takes to try to explain to Mary where the itch is.

If this machine does the trick, I could build them in quantity and put them in public places, such as restaurants and shopping malls, right next to those little machines that tell you your pulse rate for a price.

If anyone got an itch, he or she could just insert a quarter and rub until satisfied. Not only would such an invention bring me financial independence, but it would also bring sighs of happiness to lonely shoppers and diners everywhere.

The problem I haven't yet resolved is what to do with all the politicians that would be put out of work. Those people who go around smoking big cigars, wearing bright ties, and saying, "You scratch my back, I'll scratch yours," wouldn't have anything to do anymore, and then they would have to find legitimate work.

Oh, the price of progress.

52

Old Age Is an Accomplishment, Not a Handicap

As we walked into the school building, I couldn't help but wonder how many times he had done this before. After all, he had been a teacher himself for more than thirty-five years, and in the twenty years since he had retired, he had visited this place often.

Although his legs quivered a bit as we climbed the five steps up, and his hands had to hunt for the door handle that his eyes couldn't locate on first glance, his gait was steady and implied purpose.

We had come, the two of us, both seasoned veterans, to evaluate a beginning teacher. I had been coming to observe her for the past few months, but her case had me baffled. I needed help. This beginner had mastered all the skills and functions required of teaching but not the confidence. For all of her smiles and wit, there was still fear in her face where there should have been joy.

So this time, I brought an advisor with me. There were probably some who would have thought I was trying to be noble—taking out the old war-horse just to break up the monotony of his day.

The truth was that I needed something from him that I didn't have at the time—expertise seasoned with three-and-one-half decades of experience.

I wasn't disappointed. After watching the teacher more than the lesson, I delivered to her my evaluation report with that air of pomp often called professionalism.

He looked on patiently and in silence until I had finished. He then reached over, touched her hand so gently, and said, "You have such powerful teaching eyes, my dear, and you use them so well."

I could tell from the beam that spread across her countenance that he had just said something right. The deep wrinkles of fear faded away and the brightness of joy illuminated her face.

I was impressed and humbled. In one sentence he accomplished more than I had achieved in all the months I had been her advisor. I wondered why I wasn't able to do that. Could it be that I just wasn't old enough? I wasn't old enough to see her eyes or to assess their importance.

I wasn't old enough to weed through the complexity of a science to see the simplicity of an art. I wasn't old enough to touch her like he did—not in the middle of a professional evaluation report.

That afternoon I took him back to the home where he stays with others his age—out of the way and safe. I let him out at the curb and watched him totter toward the door held open by a lady in a crisp white dress.

As I sped away to urgent matters and jobs that demanded to be done that afternoon, I wondered how long I will have to live to become as accomplished as he is.